# KARMA'S COURT: THE AFTERLIFE OF INDIA'S CORRUPT OFFICIALS

**Honey Makhija**

Title : Karma's Court : The Afterlife of India's Corrupt Officials
Author : Honey Makhija
Edition : First (September, 2024)
ISBN : 9789348037497



Published by

*A Venture by -*
**PRACHI DIGITAL PUBLICATION**

Regd. Add.: 254, Khuriyakhatta No. 10, Bindukhatta,
Lalkuan, Nainital - 262402, Uttarakhand, India
Website : www.taneeshapublishers.in
E-mail : taneeshapublishers@gmail.com
Phone : +91 845481 2712, +91 976041 7980

Printed by :
Manipal Technologies Limited, Bengaluru - 560001, Karnataka

# ACKNOLEGMENMENT

I would like to express my deepest gratitude to those who have been my pillars of support throughout the journey of writing this book.

First and foremost, to my wife, Nisha—your unwavering love, patience, and encouragement have been the foundation upon which all my endeavors rest. You have been my constant companion, and your belief in me has inspired me every step of the way. To my family, whose values and teachings have shaped who I am today, I owe everything. My sisters, Kareena, Chaya, and Laveena, you have been my greatest supporters, always offering wisdom, laughter, and strength when I needed it most.

I also want to extend my heartfelt thanks to everyone at HMR Pvt Ltd. Your dedication, hard work and professionalism have not only contributed to our shared success but have also allowed me the time and space to pursue my passion for writing.

This book is as much yours as it is mine. Thank you all for being a part of this journey with me.

With sincere appreciation,

**Honey Makhija**

# INDEX

# PREFACE

In a country as diverse and complex as India, the responsibilities placed upon those in positions of power are immense. The choices made by government officials, bureaucrats, and leaders have far-reaching consequences, shaping the lives of millions of citizens. Yet, too often, the allure of power, wealth, and influence leads individuals astray, causing them to abandon the principles of honesty, integrity, and public service that should guide their actions.

This book is a narrative exploration of the moral and spiritual journey of a man who once wielded great power but lost his way in the labyrinth of corruption and self-interest. Vikram Singh, the protagonist, is not just a character; he is a symbol, a representation of the countless individuals who have succumbed to the temptations that come with authority. His story is a cautionary tale, a reminder that while one might evade earthly justice, the divine consequences of one's actions are inescapable.

The idea for this book was born out of a deep concern for the state of governance in India today. Corruption, nepotism, and the abuse of power have become pervasive issues, eroding public trust and undermining the very foundations of democracy. This is not a new problem, nor is it unique to India, but its impact on the country's progress and the well-being of its people cannot be overstated. The consequences of these actions are felt most acutely by those who are already marginalized—the poor, the vulnerable, and the voiceless.

In crafting this narrative, I sought to delve into the spiritual and moral dimensions of leadership and governance. Vikram Singh's journey through Naraka, his trials, and his ultimate rebirth as a humble servant of the people, are allegorical representations of the inner struggles faced by those in power. His story is a reflection of the potential for redemption that exists within each of us, no matter how far we may have strayed from the path of righteousness.

One of the central themes of this book is the concept of karma, the idea that every action has a corresponding consequence. In Hindu philosophy, karma is not merely punitive; it is also redemptive. It offers individuals the opportunity to atone for their past mistakes and to grow spiritually. This concept is explored in depth through Vikram's journey, as he comes to realize that his actions in life have set into motion a series of events that will ultimately determine his fate.

The book also explores the concept of dharma—righteous duty or moral law. For those in positions of power, dharma should be the guiding principle behind every decision and action. Unfortunately, in the pursuit of personal gain, many leaders lose sight of their dharma, leading to widespread corruption and injustice. Through Vikram's story, I aim to highlight the importance of adhering to dharma, not just for the sake of spiritual fulfillment, but for the betterment of society as a whole.

While this book is set in the context of Indian

society and governance, its themes are universal. The challenges of power, the temptations of corruption, and the struggle for redemption are issues that resonate across cultures and societies. The story of Vikram Singh is one that can be understood and appreciated by readers from all walks of life, regardless of their background or beliefs.

It is my hope that this book will serve as more than just a cautionary tale. I hope it will inspire reflection and self-examination among those who hold positions of authority. I hope it will encourage leaders to consider the long-term consequences of their actions, to think beyond their immediate desires, and to recognize the profound impact they have on the lives of others.

For the citizens of India, this book is a reminder of the power they hold in holding their leaders accountable. Democracy is not just about casting a vote; it is about ensuring that those who are elected to serve do so with integrity and honor. The story of Vikram Singh is a call to action, urging every Indian citizen to demand transparency, honesty, and ethical governance from those in power.

Writing this book has been a journey of introspection and learning for me. As I explored the depths of Vikram Singh's character, I found myself reflecting on my own values and beliefs. The process of writing has reinforced my conviction that true leadership is not about wielding power, but about serving others with humility and compassion. It is about making difficult choices, not for personal gain, but for the greater good.

In the course of my research, I have drawn upon a wide range of sources, including Hindu scriptures, philosophical texts, and contemporary studies on leadership and governance. These sources have provided valuable insights into the themes explored in this book, and I am grateful for the wisdom they have imparted. I have also had the privilege of engaging in conversations with individuals from various walks of life—scholars, spiritual leaders, activists, and ordinary citizens—whose perspectives have enriched my understanding of the issues at hand.

I would like to take this opportunity to express my gratitude to those who have supported me in the writing of this book. My family and friends have been a constant source of encouragement, providing me with the strength and motivation to continue even when the journey seemed difficult. I am also indebted to my editors, whose feedback and guidance have been invaluable in shaping this narrative.

As you read this book, I invite you to reflect on the themes it presents and to consider how they apply to your own life and the world around you. Whether you are a leader in government, business, or any other field, or simply a concerned citizen, I hope that Vikram Singh's story will resonate with you and inspire you to think about the choices you make and the impact they have on others.

In closing, I would like to reiterate that this book is not just a story about one man's journey. It is a reflection of the broader challenges facing our society today. It is a call to action, a plea for a return to the principles of dharma, and a reminder that true power lies not in wealth or influence, but in the ability to make a positive difference in the lives of others.

May the story of Vikram Singh serve as a beacon of light for those who seek to walk the path of righteousness, and may it inspire a new generation of leaders to embrace the values of honesty, integrity and service.

## Chapter 1

# The Final Breath of a Bureaucrat

Vikram Singh had lived a life that most would envy. He was a man of stature, a high-ranking government official who had spent decades at the helm of power. His office, nestled in the heart of New Delhi, was a fortress of luxury, shielded from the chaos of the outside world. Marble floors, expensive artwork, and antique furniture surrounded him daily, a constant reminder of the wealth and status he had accumulated over the years. But beneath the surface of this opulence lay a life built on deceit, corruption, and exploitation.

Vikram's rise to power had been anything but ordinary. He had entered the civil services with a deep sense of a6mbition, driven by the desire to escape his modest beginnings. Born to a middle-class family in a small town, Vikram had always been acutely aware of the chasm that separated the wealthy from the poor in India. His parents had instilled in him the importance of hard work and integrity, but as he climbed the bureaucratic ladder, those values became increasingly distant memories.

His first taste of corruption came early in his career. A small bribe from a contractor seeking approval for a government project had opened a door Vikram had never intended to walk through. But the money had come at a time when his family was struggling, and the temptation was too great to resist. Once the door was opened, it could never be closed again. What began as small, seemingly harmless transactions quickly escalated into a sprawling web of deceit that ensnared every aspect of his professional life.

Over the years, Vikram mastered the art of corruption. He learned how to manipulate the system to his advantage, how to curry favor with those in power, and how to hide his tracks so well that even the most diligent of investigators would find nothing amiss. His wealth grew exponentially, and with it, his influence. He became a man who could make or break careers, a kingmaker in the world of Indian bureaucracy. And yet, despite all the power and privilege, there was a part of him that was never truly at peace.

As he approached his sixtieth birthday, the shadows of his past began to weigh heavily on him. The faces of those he had wronged—farmers driven to suicide because of unpaid subsidies, families displaced by corrupt land deals, children left uneducated due to misappropriated funds—haunted him in the quiet moments when he was alone. But Vikram had always been good at pushing those thoughts aside. He justified his actions by telling himself that the system was inherently corrupt and that he was simply playing the game as it was meant to be played.

The fateful day began like any other. Vikram awoke in his sprawling bungalow in one of Delhi's most exclusive neighborhoods. The sun streamed through the floor-to-ceiling windows, casting a golden hue over the room. He stretched lazily, feeling the familiar ache in his joints that came with age, and reached for the glass of water on his bedside table. His wife, Nandini, was already up, bustling about in the kitchen, overseeing the preparations for breakfast.

As Vikram made his way to the dining room, his mind was occupied with the day's agenda. He had a series of meetings lined up—discussions with business magnates, approvals for infrastructure projects, and a private lunch with a politician who was seeking his support for an upcoming election. It was a routine day, filled with the usual mix of power plays and backroom deals. But as he sat down to breakfast, something felt off.

A sudden wave of dizziness washed over him, and he reached out to steady himself on the table. Nandini noticed immediately, her face creasing with concern.

"Are you all right, Vikram?" she asked, her voice tinged with worry.

He waved her off, attributing the dizziness to a lack of sleep. But as the day wore on, the feeling persisted. By the time he arrived at his office, the dizziness had evolved into a pounding headache, and a strange tightness gripped his chest. Still,

Vikram was not a man to let physical discomfort get in the way of his duties. He powered through his meetings, dismissing the pain as a minor inconvenience.

It wasn't until the afternoon that the situation became impossible to ignore. As he sat in his office, reviewing a stack of documents, the tightness in his chest intensified. His vision blurred, and a cold sweat broke out on his forehead. Panic set in as he realized that something was seriously wrong. He reached for the phone to call for help, but before he could dial a number, a searing pain shot through his chest, and everything went black.

Vikram collapsed onto his desk, his hand clutching his chest as he struggled to breathe. The pain was unlike anything he had ever experienced—a crushing, suffocating sensation that left him gasping for air. In those final moments, as his life slipped away, a flood of memories washed over him. He saw the faces of his parents, the pride in their eyes when he had passed the civil service exam. He saw the excitement of his first day in office, the sense of purpose he had felt. And then, he saw the darkness that had followed—the bribes, the betrayals, the countless lives ruined by his greed.

As his vision faded, Vikram was filled with an overwhelming sense of regret. He had spent his life chasing power and wealth, but in the end, none of it mattered. The mansion, the luxury cars, the offshore bank accounts—they were all meaningless in the face of death. His final breath was a whisper of despair, a silent plea for redemption that would never come.

Vikram Singh, the once-powerful bureaucrat, was no more.

The transition from life to death was instantaneous. One moment, Vikram was in his opulent office, surrounded by the trappings of power, and the next, he was enveloped in darkness. It was a darkness unlike anything he had ever known—cold, suffocating, and absolute. For what felt like an eternity, there was nothing but the void, a vast emptiness that seemed to stretch on forever.

But slowly, the darkness began to lift, replaced by a dim, flickering light. Vikram's senses returned, though they were strangely altered. He could see, but the world around him was hazy and indistinct, as if viewed through a veil. He could hear, but the sounds were distant and muffled, as though coming from the bottom of a deep well. He felt weightless, disconnected from his physical body, and yet he was acutely aware of every sensation.

As the light grew brighter, the world around him began to take shape. He found himself standing in a vast, barren landscape. The ground beneath his feet was cracked and dry, like a parched desert, and the sky above was a sickly shade of yellow, devoid of sun or clouds. There was no wind, no sound, no sign of life—just an endless expanse of emptiness that stretched as far as the eye could see.

Vikram looked down at himself and saw that he was no longer wearing the expensive suit he had donned that morning. Instead, he was clothed in simple, tattered robes, his feet bare and caked with dust. His hands, once so strong and commanding, were frail and trembling. He felt a deep, gnawing hunger in the pit of his stomach, a thirst that burned in his throat.

Panic set in as he realized the truth—he was

dead. This barren wasteland was not a dream or a hallucination; it was the afterlife, a place where the soul was stripped of all earthly possessions and left to face the consequences of its actions. Vikram's heart, or whatever semblance of a heart he had in this strange new existence, pounded with fear. He had never been a religious man, but he had heard enough stories of the afterlife to know that this was not where he wanted to be.

"Is this... hell?" he whispered to himself, his voice trembling with terror.

As if in response, a distant sound reached his ears—a low, rumbling noise that seemed to come from deep within the earth. The ground beneath him began to shake, and cracks spidered out from where he stood, widening with each passing moment. Vikram staggered back, his breath coming in short, ragged gasps as he watched in horror. From the largest of the cracks, a plume of smoke began to rise, dark and acrid, filling the air with the stench of sulfur.

Before he could react, the ground beneath him gave way entirely, and Vikram found himself falling, tumbling through the air into the darkness below. He screamed, a primal, terrified sound that echoed around him as he plummeted downward. The darkness swallowed him whole, and for a brief, agonizing moment, there was nothing but the sensation of falling, endlessly falling, with no end in sight.

But then, with a bone-jarring thud, he hit the ground. The impact knocked the breath out of him, and he lay there, gasping and disoriented, his body racked with pain. Slowly, he opened his eyes and found himself in a new environment, one that was even more terrifying than the last.

He was in a vast underground cavern, the walls lined with jagged rocks that glowed with an eerie, red light. The air was thick and oppressive, filled with the sounds of distant wailing and the clanking of chains. The ground beneath him was cold and hard, and as he struggled to his feet, he realized that he was not alone.

All around him were figures—shadowy, indistinct forms that moved slowly, shuffling through the cavern with heavy chains around their ankles. They were the souls of the damned, lost and tormented, condemned to an eternity of suffering for their sins. Some were hunched over, clutching their chests in agony, while others wandered aimlessly, their faces twisted in despair. The air was thick with the stench of decay and the acrid smell of burning flesh.

Vikram's heart raced as he took in the sight. He had heard tales of hell, of the punishment that awaited the wicked in the afterlife, but he had never truly believed them. Now, faced with the reality of it, he felt a wave of terror wash over him. Was this to be his fate? An eternity of torment, lost among the damned?

As he stood there, paralyzed with fear, a voice echoed through the cavern, deep and resonant, filled with a power that sent shivers down his spine.

**"Vikram Singh."**

The sound of his name being spoken in that voice was enough to break him out of his stupor. He turned, searching for the source, and saw a figure standing at the far end of the cavern. It was a tall, imposing figure, shrouded in darkness, with eyes that glowed like embers in the gloom. The figure stepped forward, and Vikram felt an overwhelming sense of dread as it approached.

"Who... who are you?" Vikram stammered, his voice barely above a whisper.

The figure stopped a few feet away from him, its glowing eyes boring into his soul. "I am your judge, Vikram Singh. I am the one who will decide your fate in the afterlife."

Vikram's legs trembled, and he sank to his knees, overwhelmed by the presence of this being. He had always been a man of power, a man who commanded respect and fear, but in the face of this judge, he felt utterly insignificant.

"Please," Vikram begged, his voice trembling. "I didn't mean... I didn't know...."

The judge's eyes narrowed, and a low, rumbling laugh filled the cavern. "You didn't know? You, who spent decades exploiting the powerless, who profited from the suffering of others, who betrayed the trust of those who depended on you? You didn't know?"

Vikram felt a cold sweat break out on his forehead. He had spent his life justifying his actions, convincing himself that he was simply doing what was necessary to survive, to thrive. But in the presence of this judge, all of those justifications crumbled to dust.

"You were given power," the judge continued, "and you used it to sow misery and despair. You were entrusted with the well-being of your fellow citizens, and you chose to betray that trust for your own gain. Now, you will face the consequences of your actions."

The judge raised a hand, and Vikram felt an invisible force lift him off the ground, suspending him in the air. He struggled, but it was as if his body was frozen in place, unable to move or resist. The judge's eyes burned brighter, and the cavern around them seemed to tremble with the intensity of his gaze.

"For every bribe you took, for every life you destroyed, for every injustice you allowed to flourish, you will suffer," the judge intoned. "Your soul will be weighed against the sins you have committed, and the suffering you inflicted will be returned to you a thousandfold."

Vikram's heart pounded in his chest, and he felt as though he couldn't breathe. He had never truly believed in karma, in the idea that his actions would come back to haunt him. But now, faced with the reality of it, he was consumed by a fear unlike anything he had ever known.

"Please," he gasped, his voice choked with desperation. "Give me a chance to make it right. I'll do anything, just please don't condemn me to this."

The judge's expression remained unchanged, cold and unyielding. "Your time for redemption was in the life you squandered, Vikram Singh. You had your chance, and you chose to ignore it. Now, you must face the consequences."

With a flick of the judge's hand, Vikram was thrown backward, crashing into the hard ground. He lay there, gasping for breath, his body wracked with pain. The shadows around him seemed to close in, and the sounds of wailing and despair grew louder, filling his ears with a cacophony of suffering.

As he struggled to his feet, Vikram realized with a sinking heart that there would be no escape from this place, no reprieve from the torment that awaited him. The afterlife was not a place of peace or rest; it was a realm of judgment, where every sin was weighed and every crime was punished. And for a man like him, there could be no hope of mercy.

The judge turned away, disappearing into the shadows, leaving Vikram alone in the cavern with the damned souls that surrounded him. The reality of his situation began to sink in, and he felt a crushing sense of despair. All of his power, his wealth, his influence—none of it mattered now. He was just another lost soul, condemned to an eternity of suffering for the life he had lived.

As he stood there, trembling and broken, Vikram realized that he had no one to blame but himself. He had made his choices, and now he would have to live with the consequences. The final breath of a bureaucrat was not a peaceful one; it was a breath of regret, of sorrow, of a life wasted in pursuit of all the wrong things.

And as the darkness closed in around him, Vikram knew that this was only the beginning.

## Chapter 2

# The Court of Yama

The journey through the endless darkness seemed to stretch on forever for Vikram Singh. Time had no meaning in this place, and every moment felt like an eternity. The suffocating gloom pressed in on him from all sides, and the wails of the tormented souls that surrounded him filled his ears with an incessant, maddening cacophony. His heart pounded with a dread he had never known, each beat a reminder of the unknown horrors that awaited him.

After what felt like an eternity of wandering through the bleak, desolate landscape of the afterlife, Vikram noticed a change in the atmosphere around him. The shadows that had clung to him like a second skin began to recede, and the air grew heavy with a sense of foreboding. He stopped in his tracks, every instinct telling him that something significant was about to happen.

In the distance, a faint light appeared, growing brighter with each passing moment. It wasn't the warm, comforting light that one might associate with the afterlife; instead, it was cold and unforgiving, casting long, eerie shadows that danced across the ground. The light seemed to beckon him forward, and though every fiber of his being screamed at him to turn back, he found himself drawn toward it, unable to resist its pull.

As he moved closer, the light revealed a massive structure that loomed in the distance. It was a grand, imposing palace, its walls made of dark stone that seemed to absorb the light around it. Massive pillars adorned with intricate carvings of celestial beings and fearsome demons lined the entrance, their eyes seemingly following Vikram as he approached. The air was thick with an oppressive energy, and the ground beneath his feet seemed to tremble with the weight of the place's significance.

Vikram knew, deep in his soul, that this was the Court of Yama, the Hindu god of death and justice. This was the place where souls were judged, where the deeds of a lifetime were weighed against the eternal scales of karma. He had heard of this place in stories and religious teachings, but never in his wildest dreams had he imagined he would find himself here.

As he stood before the towering entrance, the massive doors of the court creaked open with a sound that echoed through the still air. Beyond the doors lay a vast, dimly lit hall, its ceiling so high that it seemed to vanish into the darkness above. The floor was made of smooth black marble, reflecting the light of the torches that lined the walls. The atmosphere was heavy with a sense of solemnity and judgment, and Vikram could feel the weight of a thousand unseen eyes upon him.

With hesitant steps, he crossed the threshold and entered the hall. The doors slammed shut behind him with a resounding boom, sealing him inside. Vikram's heart raced as he walked deeper into the hall, his footsteps echoing off the walls. At the far end of the hall, he could make out a raised platform, upon which sat a massive, ornate throne. The throne was carved from black stone and adorned with gold and jewels, its grandeur a stark contrast to the austere surroundings.

Seated upon the throne was Yama, the god of death and justice. He was an imposing figure, towering over Vikram even from a distance. Yama's skin was a deep shade of blue, and his eyes burned with an intense, otherworldly light. He wore a crown of gold and a flowing robe of dark fabric that seemed to shimmer with an inner light. In one hand, he held a staff topped with a skull, a symbol of his dominion over life and death. In the other, he held a set of scales, the scales of justice upon which every soul would be weighed.

At Yama's feet sat two figures, each with a massive scroll unfurled before them. These were Chitragupta and his twin brother Yama-Kinkara, the divine accountants who meticulously recorded the deeds of every soul that passed through the mortal world. Their faces were inscrutable, their eyes never leaving the scrolls as they scribbled down every detail with a quill made from a single black feather.

Vikram's legs trembled as he approached the throne, his body betraying the fear that gripped his soul. He had faced powerful men in his lifetime, men who commanded armies and controlled vast fortunes, but never had he felt as small and insignificant as he did in this moment. The weight of his sins pressed down on him like a physical burden, and he knew that there would be no escape from the judgment that awaited him.

As he came to a stop before the throne, Yama's gaze fell upon him, and Vikram felt as though the god's eyes were piercing through to the very core of his being. The intensity of Yama's gaze was unbearable, and Vikram found himself trembling uncontrollably, unable to meet the god's eyes.

"Vikram Singh," Yama's voice echoed through the hall, deep and resonant, filled with an authority that left no room for doubt. "You stand before this court to answer for the deeds of your life. Do you understand the gravity of this moment?"

Vikram's throat was dry, and he struggled to find his voice. "Yes... I understand," he managed to croak out, his voice barely above a whisper.

Yama nodded, his expression unreadable. "Your life will be laid bare before this court. Every action, every thought, every intention will be weighed against the scales of karma. There is no hiding from the truth here, Vikram Singh. The divine accountants have recorded everything."

At Yama's command, Chitragupta and Yama-Kinkara began to read from their scrolls. The sound of their voices filled the hall, a relentless recitation of every act of corruption, every bribe, every betrayal that Vikram had committed in his life. Each word was like a hammer blow, shattering the fragile defenses that Vikram had built up over the years to justify his actions.

They spoke of the early years, when Vikram had first entered the civil services, full of ambition and the desire to make a difference. But it wasn't long before the allure of power and wealth began to corrupt him. They recounted the first bribe he took—a small sum, but it was enough to set him on a path of dishonesty. From that point on, the floodgates were open, and Vikram's life became a tangled web of deceit.

The scrolls revealed how he had manipulated the system for his own gain, how he had used his position to amass a fortune while turning a blind eye to the suffering of others. The stories of the farmers driven to suicide by his refusal to release subsidies, the families displaced by his corrupt land deals, and the children deprived of education because of misappropriated funds were laid bare for all to see. Each account was more damning than the last, a testament to the extent of his moral decay.

As the recitation continued, Vikram's mind was filled with images of those he had wronged. He saw the faces of the farmers, their eyes hollow with despair as they faced the loss of their livelihoods. He saw the tears of the families who had been thrown out of their homes, their lives shattered by his greed. He saw the children, their futures stolen from them, forced into lives of poverty because of his corruption.

With each revelation, Vikram's heart grew heavier, weighed down by the enormity of his sins. He had always known that his actions were wrong, but he had convinced himself that it was the way of the world, that everyone in his position did the same. He had buried his guilt beneath layers of justification and denial, but now, in the presence of Yama, there was no escape from the truth.

As the divine accountants continued their recitation, they spoke of the moments when Vikram could have chosen a different path. There were times when he had been presented with opportunities to make amends, to turn away from the corruption that had consumed him, but he had ignored them, choosing instead to dig himself deeper into the mire of dishonesty. He had been given chances to seek redemption, to atone for his sins, but he had let them slip through his fingers, blinded by his hunger for power and wealth.

Finally, after what felt like an eternity, the recitation came to an end. The hall fell silent, the weight of Vikram's sins hanging heavy in the air. Yama's eyes bore into him, and Vikram felt as though his very soul was being laid bare before the god.

"Vikram Singh," Yama said, his voice devoid of emotion. "You have heard the account of your life. You have seen the suffering you have caused, the lives you have destroyed in your pursuit of power. Do you have anything to say in your defense?"

Vikram's mouth opened and closed, but no words came out. What could he say? How could he defend the indefensible? Every excuse he had ever made for his actions sounded hollow and meaningless in the face of the truth. He had spent his life hiding from the consequences of his actions, but now there was no hiding. The truth was laid bare, and there was no escape from it.

"I... I was wrong," Vikram finally managed to say, his voice trembling. "I know that now. I see the pain I caused, the lives I ruined. I was blinded by greed, by ambition... I don't know what else to say."

Yama's gaze remained fixed on him, unblinking and unyielding. "Words are easy, Vikram Singh. They are not enough to undo the harm you have done. You had a lifetime to make different choices, to seek redemption, but you chose to ignore those opportunities. Now, you must face the consequences."

With a wave of his hand, Yama summoned the scales of justice, the golden balance hovering in the air before him. The scales were no ordinary object; they were imbued with the power to measure the true weight of a soul, to balance the good and evil deeds of a lifetime against one another. It was said that the scales were infallible, that they could not be deceived or manipulated. They would reveal the true nature of a soul, and there would be no escape from their judgment.

Yama placed a single black feather on one side of the scale, representing Vikram's good deeds. The feather was light as air, barely enough to tip the balance. On the other side, Chitragupta and Yama-Kinkara placed the weight of Vikram's sins—a heavy, dark mass that seemed to pull the scale down with an inexorable force.

The scales tipped sharply under the weight of Vikram's sins, the feather barely making a dent in the balance. Vikram watched in despair as the scale continued to tip further and further, the weight of his sins dragging it down into darkness. The sight filled him with a sense of hopelessness, of utter defeat. He had known, deep down, that his sins outweighed his good deeds, but seeing it laid out before him in such stark terms was a blow that he had not been prepared for.

Yama's voice broke the silence, the final judgment hanging in the air like a death sentence. "Vikram Singh, your soul has been weighed, and it has been found wanting. Your sins far outweigh any good you have done in your life. The suffering you have caused will be returned to you, and you will be condemned to an eternity in Naraka, the realm of torment for the wicked."

Vikram's heart sank at the pronouncement, a wave of despair washing over him. He had heard stories of Naraka, the hellish realm where souls were tormented for their sins, where there was no escape from the pain and suffering that awaited them. It was a place of unimaginable horrors, where the worst of humanity was punished for their deeds. And now, it was his fate, the final destination for his corrupted soul.

"No... please," Vikram begged, falling to his knees before the god. "There must be something I can do, some way to make amends. I don't want to go to Naraka... please, give me a chance to make things right."

But Yama's expression remained cold and

unmoved. "You had your chances, Vikram Singh. In life, you were given opportunities to change your path, to seek redemption, but you ignored them. Now, it is too late. The consequences of your actions cannot be undone."

With another wave of his hand, Yama summoned two of his attendants, fierce-looking beings with dark skin and glowing eyes. They stepped forward, their hands gripping chains that rattled ominously as they approached Vikram. The chains were no ordinary bonds; they were imbued with the power to bind the soul, to drag it down into the depths of Naraka, where it would face the full weight of its sins.

Vikram tried to struggle, but it was futile. The attendants bound him in the chains, the cold metal biting into his flesh as they tightened around him. He could feel the weight of the chains pulling him down, as if they were dragging him into the very depths of the earth. Panic seized him, and he thrashed against the bonds, but there was no escape.

As the attendants began to drag him away, Vikram

cast one last desperate look at Yama, hoping against hope for some reprieve, some sign of mercy. But Yama's expression remained unchanged, as cold and distant as ever. There would be no mercy, no escape from the judgment that had been passed.

The attendants pulled Vikram through the hall, the chains rattling with each step. The walls seemed to close in around him, the air growing colder and heavier with every passing moment. The wails of the damned souls echoed in his ears, a haunting chorus that filled him with dread. He knew that soon, he would be one of them, lost in the endless torment of Naraka.

As they reached the far end of the hall, Vikram saw a massive, iron-bound door set into the wall. The door was ancient, its surface covered in strange, arcane symbols that seemed to pulse with a dark energy. The attendants pushed the door open, and a blast of cold, foul-smelling air rushed out, carrying with it the sounds of distant screams and the stench of decay.

Beyond the door lay a vast, dark abyss, the entrance to Naraka. It was a place of eternal night, where the only light came from the flickering flames that licked at the edges of the abyss, casting eerie shadows on the walls. The ground was littered with jagged rocks and bones, and the air was thick with the scent of burning flesh.

Vikram's heart pounded with terror as he was dragged to the edge of the abyss. He could see no bottom, only an endless void that seemed to stretch on forever. The thought of being cast into that darkness, of spending eternity in the torment of Naraka, filled him with a despair that was beyond anything he had ever known.

"No... please, no," he begged, his voice choked with fear. "Don't send me there... I'll do anything, just please don't send me there."

But his pleas fell on deaf ears. The attendants tightened their grip on the chains, and with one final, forceful shove, they pushed Vikram over the edge.

Vikram's scream echoed through the abyss as he fell, the darkness swallowing him whole. The last thing he saw before he was consumed by the void was the cold, unforgiving eyes of Yama, watching him as he plummeted into the depths.

And then, there was nothing. Only darkness, and the endless, unrelenting torment of Naraka.

The Court of Yama had passed its judgment, and there would be no escape for Vikram Singh. The consequences of his life of corruption had finally caught up with him, and now, he would face the full weight of his sins in the afterlife.

As he fell deeper into the abyss, the reality of his situation began to sink in. There was no more power, no more wealth, no more influence. All that remained was the cold, hard truth of his actions, and the suffering that awaited him in the depths of Naraka.

The final breath of a bureaucrat had led him to this place, and there would be no escape from the judgment that had been passed.

In the end, all that was left was darkness.

## *Chapter 3*

# The Danda of Chitragupta

Vikram Singh's fall into the abyss felt like an eternity. The darkness consumed him, pressing in from all sides, suffocating him with the weight of his sins. His screams echoed through the void, swallowed by the blackness that surrounded him. There was no sense of time or space, no ground beneath his feet, no sky above his head—only the endless, terrifying descent into Naraka.

Finally, the fall came to an abrupt end. Vikram crashed into the cold, hard ground with a force that knocked the breath out of him. He lay there for a moment, dazed and disoriented, his body aching from the impact. The air was thick and heavy, filled with the stench of decay and the distant sounds of wailing and despair.

Slowly, he opened his eyes and found himself in a vast, desolate wasteland. The ground was cracked and barren, the earth scorched and lifeless. The sky above was a sickly shade of red, devoid of any sun or stars, casting an eerie glow over the landscape. The only light came from the flickering flames that dotted the horizon, their orange and yellow tongues licking at the edges of the darkness.

Vikram struggled to his feet, his body trembling with fear and exhaustion. His clothes were torn and ragged, his skin bruised and battered. He felt a deep, gnawing hunger in the pit of his stomach, a thirst that burned in his throat. Every part of him ached, and the cold, unrelenting dread that had taken hold of him in the Court of Yama only intensified.

As he looked around, he saw the twisted, tormented forms of other souls wandering aimlessly through the wasteland. They were shadows of their former selves, their faces gaunt and hollow, their eyes filled with despair. Some were chained to the ground, their limbs twisted and contorted, while others were consumed by flames that seemed to burn without end. Their cries of agony echoed through the air, a chorus of suffering that sent shivers down Vikram's spine.

This was Naraka, the realm of torment for the

wicked. The place where the consequences of a life lived in sin were fully realized, where there was no escape from the suffering that awaited. Vikram had heard of this place in religious teachings, but nothing could have prepared him for the reality of it. The tales of endless suffering, of torment that stretched on for eternity, were no longer just stories—they were his new reality.

As he stood there, trying to comprehend the horrors that surrounded him, Vikram heard a voice—a deep, resonant voice that seemed to come from everywhere and nowhere at once.

"Vikram Singh."

He froze, his heart pounding in his chest. He recognized the voice; it was the same voice that had spoken to him in the Court of Yama. But this time, there was something different about it—something even more ominous.

**"Come forward," the voice commanded.**

Vikram hesitated, his legs trembling with fear. But he knew that there was no point in resisting. There was no escape from this place, no refuge from the judgment that awaited him. He took a deep breath and began to walk toward the source of the voice, his footsteps echoing off the cracked ground.

As he walked, the landscape around him began to change. The barren wasteland gave way to a vast, dark chamber, its walls lined with jagged rocks that seemed to pulse with a faint, red glow. The air grew colder, and Vikram felt a chill run down his spine as he stepped into the chamber.

At the far end of the chamber stood a tall, imposing figure, his form shrouded in darkness. In his hand, he held a long staff, its surface carved with intricate symbols that seemed to writhe and twist in the dim light. The staff was the danda of Chitragupta, the divine scribe and keeper of records, the instrument of justice used to deliver punishment to the wicked.

Vikram's breath caught in his throat as he realized who stood before him. Chitragupta was the scribe of Yama, the god of death and justice, and it was his duty to record the deeds of every soul that passed through the mortal world. He was the one who had meticulously documented every bribe, every act of corruption, every betrayal that Vikram had committed in his life. And now, he was here to deliver the punishment that Vikram so rightly deserved.

Chitragupta's eyes glowed with an otherworldly light as he looked down at Vikram, his expression cold and unyielding. There was no pity in those eyes, no compassion—only the harsh, unforgiving judgment of a divine being who had seen the worst of humanity.

"Vikram Singh," Chitragupta's voice echoed through the chamber, "you have been brought here to face the consequences of your actions. The suffering you inflicted on others in life will now be returned to you. The danda will serve as the instrument of your punishment, stripping away the illusions of power and control that you clung to in life."

Vikram's legs gave way, and he collapsed to his knees before the scribe, his body trembling with fear. He had never felt so helpless, so utterly powerless. The weight of his sins pressed down on him, suffocating him with the knowledge of what was to come.

"Please," Vikram begged, his voice shaking, "I

didn't know... I didn't mean to cause so much pain...."

But Chitragupta's expression remained unchanged, his eyes cold and unyielding. "Ignorance is no excuse, Vikram Singh. You were given the power to help others, to serve your fellow man, but you chose to use that power for your own gain. You turned a blind eye to the suffering of others, and now you will face the consequences of those choices."

With a slow, deliberate motion, Chitragupta raised the danda above his head. The staff seemed to pulse with a dark energy, the symbols on its surface glowing with a sinister light. Vikram watched in horror as the staff descended toward him, its power drawing closer with every passing moment.

And then, with a resounding crack, the danda struck him.

The pain was immediate and overwhelming. It was as though every nerve in his body had been set on fire, the agony searing through him with an intensity that left him gasping for breath. His vision blurred, and for a moment, he thought he might lose consciousness, but the pain was too strong, too relentless to allow him even that small mercy.

As the pain coursed through him, Vikram's mind was filled with images—images of the people he had wronged, the lives he had destroyed through his corruption. He saw the faces of the farmers who had been driven to suicide because of his refusal to release subsidies. Their eyes were hollow, their faces gaunt and lined with despair as they faced the loss of their livelihoods. He heard their voices, pleading with him for help, but he had turned them away, choosing to protect his own interests instead.

The danda struck him again, and the pain intensified, tearing through him like a white-hot blade. More images filled his mind—families who had been displaced by his corrupt land deals, their homes destroyed, their lives shattered. He saw the tears of the children who had been forced to live on the streets, their futures stolen from them because of his greed. He heard the cries of the mothers who had lost their children, their voices filled with anguish and despair.

Each blow from the danda was a reminder of the suffering he had caused, a punishment that cut through the layers of justification and denial he had built up over the years. There was no escape from the truth now, no refuge from the guilt that gnawed at his soul. The illusions of power and control that he had clung to in life were stripped away, leaving him exposed, vulnerable, and utterly alone.

As the danda continued to strike him, Vikram felt a profound sense of despair wash over him. He had spent his life convincing himself that he was untouchable, that his wealth and influence would protect him from the consequences of his actions. But now, faced with the harsh reality of his sins, he realized just how wrong he had been.

The danda was relentless, each blow stripping away another layer of his soul, leaving him raw and exposed. The pain was beyond anything he had ever imagined, a torment that seemed to go on forever, with no end in sight. He felt as though he was being torn apart from the inside, his very essence unraveling under the weight of his sins.

And yet, even as the pain consumed him, there was a part of Vikram that clung to the hope that it would end, that there would be some reprieve from the torment. But Chitragupta's expression remained cold and unyielding, and Vikram knew that there would be no mercy, no escape from the punishment that awaited him.

Finally, after what felt like an eternity, the blows ceased. Vikram lay on the ground, his body trembling with pain, his breath coming in short, ragged gasps. The chamber was silent, the only sound the faint echo of his own labored breathing.

Chitragupta lowered the danda, his eyes still fixed on Vikram. "The pain you feel now is only a fraction of the suffering you caused in life, Vikram Singh. The danda is not merely a tool of punishment; it is a symbol of justice, a reminder that no one is above the law. Your actions have consequences, and those consequences must be faced."

Vikram's voice was weak, barely a whisper as he spoke. "I'm sorry... I'm so sorry...."

But Chitragupta shook his head. "Sorry is not enough. Words cannot undo the harm you have done. The suffering of those you wronged cannot be erased by mere apologies. You must atone for your sins, and that atonement will come through the punishment you now face."

As Vikram lay there, broken and defeated, Chitragupta raised the danda once more. This time, however, the staff did not strike him. Instead, it hovered above him, its power radiating through the chamber.

"Your punishment is not yet complete, Vikram Singh," Chitragupta said, his voice filled with a solemn gravity. "There are still those who must have their voices heard, those who were silenced by your actions in life. You will now confront the souls of those who suffered because of your corruption. They will speak, and you will listen. And with each testimony, the danda will deliver the justice you deserve."

With a wave of his hand, Chitragupta summoned the first of the souls. A figure materialized before Vikram, a man with a weathered face and hollow eyes, his expression filled with sorrow and anger. Vikram recognized him immediately—he was one of the farmers who had taken his own life because of the crushing debt he had been unable to repay, a debt that Vikram had refused to forgive.

The farmer's voice was steady, but there was a deep pain behind his words. "I came to you for help, Vikram Singh. I begged you to release the funds that were rightfully ours, the subsidies that would have saved my land, my family. But you turned me away. You told me there was nothing you could do, that the system was to blame. But I knew the truth. I knew that you had the power to help, but you chose not to."

As the farmer spoke, the danda descended once more, striking Vikram with a force that left him gasping for breath. The pain was unbearable, a searing agony that cut through him like a knife. But the farmer continued, his voice unwavering.

"I lost everything because of you," the farmer said, his voice filled with a quiet rage. "My land, my home, my family... all gone because of your greed, your corruption. And when I could take no more, when the weight of it all became too much to bear, I ended my life. But even in death, there was no peace for me, no escape from the suffering you caused."

The danda struck again, the pain even more intense than before. Vikram's body convulsed with the force of the blow, his mind reeling from the onslaught of guilt and despair.

One by one, the souls of those Vikram had wronged came forward to speak. There were the families who had been displaced by his corrupt land deals, their homes destroyed to make way for projects that never materialized. There were the children who had been deprived of an education because of the funds he had embezzled, their futures stolen from them before they had even begun. Each testimony was a fresh wound, each blow from the danda a reminder of the suffering he had caused.

As the souls continued to speak, Vikram's mind was overwhelmed with the weight of his sins. He had always known that his actions were wrong, but he had convinced himself that they were necessary, that he was simply doing what was required to survive in a corrupt system. But now, faced with the reality of the pain he had inflicted on others, those justifications crumbled to dust.

The danda continued to strike him, each blow stripping away another layer of his soul, leaving him raw and exposed. The pain was unbearable, a torment that seemed to go on forever, with no end in sight. Vikram felt as though he was being torn apart from the inside, his very essence unraveling under the weight of his sins.

Finally, after what felt like an eternity, the last of the souls stepped forward. It was a child, no more than six years old, her face gaunt and pale, her eyes filled with a sorrow that no child should ever have to bear. Vikram's heart broke at the sight of her, the guilt overwhelming him as he realized who she was.

The child's voice was soft, but there was a strength in it that belied her small frame. "You took everything from me, Vikram Singh. My home, my family, my future... all gone because of you. I was just a child, but you didn't care. You saw only the money, the power, and you took it all, leaving nothing for me."

The danda descended one final time, and Vikram felt as though his soul was being ripped from his body. The pain was beyond anything he had ever imagined, a torment that left him gasping for breath, his body convulsing with the force of the blow.

As the child finished speaking, the chamber fell

silent. The souls of those Vikram had wronged faded into the darkness, their voices lingering in the air, a haunting reminder of the suffering he had caused.

Chitragupta lowered the danda, his expression cold and unyielding. "The punishment you have faced here is only the beginning, Vikram Singh. Your journey through Naraka will continue, and with each step, you will confront the consequences of your actions. The suffering you inflicted on others will be returned to you, and there will be no escape, no reprieve from the justice that awaits."

Vikram lay on the ground, broken and defeated, his body trembling with pain, his mind overwhelmed with guilt and despair. The chamber around him seemed to close in, the darkness pressing in from all sides, suffocating him with the weight of his sins.

As Chitragupta turned to leave, Vikram's voice, weak and trembling, called out to him. "Is there no hope for redemption? No chance for forgiveness?"

Chitragupta paused, his eyes fixed on Vikram. "Redemption is not given, Vikram Singh. It must be earned. The path you have chosen is one of suffering, but through that suffering, there may be a chance for atonement. The journey will be long and difficult, and there are no guarantees. But if you truly seek redemption, you must face the full weight of your sins and make amends for the harm you have caused."

With those final words, Chitragupta turned and disappeared into the darkness, leaving Vikram alone in the chamber, the echoes of the danda's blows still ringing in his ears.

Vikram's body trembled with pain, his mind reeling from the torment he had endured. The suffering he had inflicted on others had been returned to him in full, and he knew that his journey through Naraka was far from over. There would be more trials, more punishments, more confrontations with the souls of those he had wronged.

But as he lay there, broken and defeated, a small spark of hope flickered within him. Perhaps, just perhaps, there was a chance for redemption. It would not be easy, and the road ahead would be filled with suffering, but if there was even the slightest possibility of atoning for his sins, he would take it.

With great effort, Vikram forced himself to his feet, his body trembling with pain and exhaustion. The chamber around him was silent, the darkness pressing in from all sides, but he knew that he could not stay here. There was a journey ahead of him, a path he had to walk, no matter how difficult it might be.

And so, with a heavy heart and a soul weighed down by guilt, Vikram Singh took his first steps on the path to redemption, leaving the chamber of Chitragupta behind. The road ahead was long and filled with suffering, but for the first time in his life, he understood the true weight of his actions and the price he would have to pay to atone for them.

The danda had delivered its justice, and now, it was up to Vikram to face the consequences.

## *Chapter 4*

# The Naraka of Greed

Vikram Singh's journey through the afterlife was far from over. Each step he took away from the chamber of Chitragupta seemed to lead him deeper into the darkness, the oppressive weight of his sins pressing down on him with every breath. The pain from the blows of the danda still lingered, a constant reminder of the suffering he had inflicted on others and the justice that awaited him.

As he walked, the landscape around him began to change. The barren wasteland of Naraka gave way to a new, more sinister environment. The ground beneath his feet turned to cold, hard stone, and the air grew thick with the stench of decay and rot. The once distant wails of the damned grew louder, filling the air with a cacophony of anguish that seemed to reverberate through Vikram's very soul.

Before him loomed a massive, jagged mountain, its peak shrouded in dark, swirling clouds. The path leading up the mountain was narrow and treacherous, lined with sharp rocks that seemed to jut out at impossible angles. The mountain itself appeared alive, its surface pulsating with a sinister energy that sent shivers down Vikram's spine.

He knew, instinctively, that this was his next destination—the Naraka of Greed, a realm specifically designed to torment those who had spent their lives consumed by an insatiable hunger for wealth and power. It was a place where the very desires that had driven Vikram in life would be turned against him, where he would be forced to confront the emptiness that lay at the heart of his greed.

With a heavy heart and trembling hands, Vikram began the ascent up the mountain. Each step was a struggle, the path steep and unforgiving. The sharp rocks cut into his feet, drawing blood with every movement, but the pain was nothing compared to the dread that filled him as he climbed higher and higher.

As he neared the summit, the air grew colder, and a thick, cloying mist began to envelop the path. The mist was dense, almost suffocating, and with every breath, Vikram felt as though he was inhaling the very essence of his own greed. The sensation was overwhelming, a gnawing hunger that seemed to claw at his insides, urging him to continue onward despite the pain and exhaustion.

Finally, after what felt like an eternity of climbing, Vikram reached the summit. The peak of the mountain was a vast, barren plateau, its surface littered with the remnants of shattered dreams and broken promises. The ground was strewn with gold coins, glittering jewels, and other symbols of wealth and power, but they were tarnished and dull, their luster long since faded.

In the center of the plateau stood a massive throne, carved from black stone and adorned with the spoils of countless lives ruined by greed. The throne was empty, but its presence was palpable, a symbol of the ultimate prize that Vikram had spent his life chasing—the seat of power, the pinnacle of wealth, the object of his deepest desires.

But as he approached the throne, Vikram realized with a sinking heart that something was terribly wrong. The closer he got, the more the throne seemed to recede into the distance, always just out of reach. No matter how fast he walked, no matter how desperately he tried to grasp it, the throne remained elusive, taunting him with the promise of wealth and power that would never be his.

Vikram's heart pounded with frustration and desperation. He had spent his entire life in pursuit of wealth and power, and now, in the afterlife, those same desires were being used to torment him. The more he reached out for the throne, the more it slipped away from him, leaving him with nothing but the gnawing emptiness that had driven him to this place.

As he continued to chase the throne, the landscape around him began to shift. The gold coins and jewels at his feet turned to dust, crumbling beneath his touch. The mist thickened, swirling around him like a living entity, whispering in his ear, feeding his greed, urging him to continue the pursuit. The more he reached for the throne, the more he felt the hunger inside him grow, a relentless, all-consuming desire that threatened to devour him whole.

And then, as if in response to his desperation, the throne began to transform. The black stone cracked and crumbled, revealing a twisted, grotesque figure seated upon it. The figure was a mirror image of Vikram himself, but twisted and distorted by greed. Its eyes gleamed with a malevolent hunger, its hands clutching at the arms of the throne with a ferocity that sent shivers down Vikram's spine.

The figure grinned, a cruel, mocking smile that revealed rows of sharp, jagged teeth. "You want this, don't you?" it hissed, its voice a twisted echo of Vikram's own. "You've always wanted this—the power, the wealth, the control. But no matter how hard you try, it will always be just out of reach, slipping through your fingers like sand."

Vikram recoiled in horror, the realization of what he had become crashing down on him like a tidal wave. He had spent his life chasing after wealth and power, believing that they would bring him happiness, fulfillment, and security. But now, faced with the twisted reflection of his own greed, he saw the truth for what it was—an endless, insatiable hunger that could never be satisfied.

The figure on the throne leaned forward, its eyes gleaming with a sinister light. "You will spend eternity here, chasing after what you desire most, but you will never have it. The more you grasp, the more it will slip away from you, leaving you with nothing but the emptiness inside you. This is the Naraka of Greed, where the greedy are tormented by their own desires, forever chasing what they can never attain."

Vikram fell to his knees, his body trembling with fear and despair. The hunger inside him gnawed at his insides, a relentless, all-consuming force that drove him to reach out once more for the throne, even though he knew it would only bring him more pain. The figure on the throne watched him with a cruel, mocking grin, its eyes gleaming with satisfaction as Vikram's hands clawed at the ground, desperate to grasp the wealth and power that would forever elude him.

And so, the torment began.

In the Naraka of Greed, time had no meaning. Days, weeks, months—all of it blurred together in an endless cycle of torment and frustration.

Vikram spent every waking moment chasing after the throne, driven by the insatiable hunger that consumed him. The more he reached out, the more the throne slipped away from him, leaving him with nothing but the empty, gnawing void inside.

The landscape around him shifted constantly, the ground crumbling beneath his feet, the mist swirling around him like a living entity. The throne remained ever elusive, always just out of reach, taunting him with the promise of wealth and power that would never be his.

Vikram's body grew weaker with each passing moment, his muscles aching from the relentless pursuit, his mind fraying under the weight of his desires. But no matter how exhausted he became, the hunger inside him never waned. It was a relentless, all-consuming force that drove him to continue the chase, even as his body and soul were slowly torn apart by the torment.

There were moments when Vikram tried to resist the hunger, to stop himself from reaching out for the throne. But the emptiness inside him was too great, the desire too overwhelming. The figure on the throne watched him with cruel amusement, its eyes gleaming with satisfaction as Vikram's resolve crumbled, and he succumbed once more to the relentless pursuit of his desires.

The torment was unending, a never-ending cycle of frustration and despair. Vikram's hands were raw and bloody from clawing at the ground, his body battered and bruised from the constant chase. The figure on the throne remained ever-present, a twisted reflection of his own greed, mocking him with every failed attempt to grasp what he desired most.

And yet, despite the torment, there was no escape. The hunger inside him was too strong, the emptiness too great. No matter how many times he tried to resist, he always found himself reaching out once more, driven by the insatiable desire that had consumed him in life and now tormented him in death.

As the torment continued, Vikram began to lose track of time. The days blurred together in an endless haze of pain and frustration, the landscape around him shifting and changing with every failed attempt to grasp the throne. The mist swirled around him, whispering in his ear, feeding his greed, urging him to continue the pursuit.

But with each passing moment, Vikram's mind began to fray. The constant cycle of torment and frustration was too much for him to bear, the endless hunger too overwhelming. He began to lose himself in the madness, his thoughts consumed by the desire for wealth and power, his mind fraying under the weight of his own greed.

The figure on the throne watched him with a cruel, mocking grin, its eyes gleaming with satisfaction as Vikram's mind began to unravel. The hunger inside him grew stronger, driving him to continue the pursuit, even as his body and soul were slowly torn apart by the torment.

And then, one day—though in this place, the concept of day and night was meaningless—something changed. The mist that had swirled around Vikram for so long began to dissipate, revealing the landscape in stark clarity. The throne that had been ever-elusive seemed to grow more solid, more real, and Vikram's desperation reached new heights.

Driven by a sudden surge of hope, Vikram lunged for the throne with every ounce of strength he had left. His hands reached out, fingers outstretched, as he strained to grasp the object of his desires. For a brief, fleeting moment, it seemed as though he might finally succeed. His fingertips brushed the edge of the throne, and his heart soared with a sense of triumph.

But just as quickly as the hope had come, it was dashed. The throne shattered into a thousand pieces, crumbling to dust in his hands. The mist swirled around him once more, enveloping him in its cold embrace, and Vikram was left kneeling on the ground, his hands clutching at nothing but air.

The emptiness inside him yawned wider than ever, a vast, bottomless pit that threatened to consume him entirely. The hunger that had driven him to this point was now a living, breathing thing, gnawing at his insides, devouring him from within. The figure on the throne, or what remained of it, laughed—a cruel, mocking sound that echoed through the desolate landscape.

"You will never have it, Vikram Singh," the figure taunted, its voice dripping with malice. "No matter how hard you try, no matter how desperately you chase after it, you will never have what you desire most. You will spend eternity here, grasping at shadows, consumed by a hunger that can never be satisfied."

Vikram collapsed to the ground, his body trembling with exhaustion and despair. The realization that he would never escape this torment, that he would be trapped in this endless cycle of desire and frustration for all eternity, was too much to bear. The hunger inside him was a living nightmare, a constant reminder of the emptiness that had driven him to this place.

As he lay there, broken and defeated, the mist began to close in around him, obscuring the landscape once more. The figure on the throne faded into the darkness, its mocking laughter echoing in Vikram's ears as the last remnants of hope were stripped away.

The Naraka of Greed was a place of endless torment, where the very desires that had driven

Vikram in life were turned against him, used to torture him for all eternity. There was no escape from the hunger, no reprieve from the emptiness that gnawed at his soul. The more he grasped, the more it eluded him, leaving him with nothing but the hollow void inside.

And so, Vikram's torment continued, an endless cycle of frustration and despair. The Naraka of Greed had claimed him, and there would be no escape from the torment that awaited him. The hunger that had driven him in life now consumed him in death, an insatiable force that would never be satisfied.

As the mist closed in around him, Vikram felt the last remnants of his sanity slipping away. The hunger inside him was all that remained, a living nightmare that would haunt him for all eternity. The Naraka of Greed was his final destination, the place where his sins had led him, and there would be no escape from the torment that awaited him.

The throne, the wealth, the power—everything he had desired in life was now nothing but a distant memory, a cruel reminder of the emptiness that had driven him to this place. The more he grasped, the more it slipped away, leaving him with nothing but the endless, insatiable hunger that would torment him for all eternity.

And so, Vikram Singh, once a powerful bureaucrat, now a soul lost in the Naraka of Greed, continued his endless pursuit, forever chasing after what he could never attain. The torment was unending, the hunger insatiable, and the emptiness all-consuming. This was his fate, the price of his greed, and there would be no escape.

The Naraka of Greed had claimed him, and there would be no end to his suffering.

## Chapter 5

# The River of Sins

The cold waters of the Vaitarna River churned with a life of their own, dark and malevolent. The surface seemed to writhe with shadows, the accumulated sins of the dead woven into the very essence of the river. Vikram Singh stood at the edge, the echoes of the Naraka of Greed still fresh in his mind, his soul burdened with the weight of his past misdeeds. The air was thick with tension, a heavy atmosphere that seemed to press down on him, making it difficult to breathe.

He knew what awaited him. The Vaitarna River was not merely a physical challenge; it was a trial of the soul, a crossing that would force him to confront the full measure of the suffering he had caused in life. To reach the other side, he would have to endure the pain and despair of those he had wronged, to feel their anguish as if it were his own.

With a trembling hand, Vikram took his first step

into the river.

The water was icy cold, a shock that sent shivers down his spine. But as he waded deeper, the temperature began to change. The cold gave way to a burning heat, as if the water itself was a liquid fire, scorching his skin, searing his flesh. The pain was immediate and overwhelming, but it was nothing compared to what came next.

As the water reached his knees, Vikram felt a strange sensation beneath the surface. It was as if something was moving in the water, brushing against his legs, tugging at him with unseen hands. Panic set in, and he tried to pull back, but the current was too strong, dragging him deeper into the river.

The first of the souls emerged from the water, a ghostly figure with hollow eyes and a twisted expression of pain. It was the specter of a farmer, one of the many whose lives had been destroyed by Vikram's corruption. The farmer's face was etched with lines of despair, his hands gnarled and worn from years of toil that had led to nothing but ruin.

"You took everything from me," the farmer's voice echoed in the still air, a haunting whisper that seemed to resonate deep within Vikram's soul. "My land, my family, my hope... all gone because of you."

Vikram tried to speak, to defend himself, but the words caught in his throat. The farmer's hands reached out, grasping Vikram's arms with a strength that belied their frail appearance. The touch was cold, and as the farmer's grip tightened, Vikram felt a surge of pain, not just in his body, but in his very soul. It was as if the farmer's anguish was being transferred to him, a burden that he could not escape.

"You promised us help," the farmer continued, his voice rising with emotion. "You promised us a future, and instead, you left us with nothing. My children starved, my wife died of despair, and I... I took my own life, because there was nothing left for me."

With each word, the pain in Vikram's chest grew more intense, a burning ache that spread through his entire body. He could feel the farmer's despair, the hopelessness that had driven him to end his life, and it was almost too much to bear. The weight of the farmer's suffering was crushing, a suffocating force that left Vikram gasping for breath.

But the river showed no mercy.

The current surged, pulling Vikram deeper into the water. The farmer's grip loosened, and he was swept away, disappearing beneath the surface. But as soon as he was gone, another figure emerged, this one a woman with hollow eyes and a face twisted in sorrow.

Vikram recognized her immediately. She was one of the many young women he had exploited during his time in power, using his influence to take what he wanted, without a thought for the consequences. Her life had been shattered by his actions, her future stolen, her dreams destroyed.

"You took my dignity," the woman's voice was a soft, broken whisper, filled with a sadness that pierced Vikram's heart. "You took everything from me, and left me with nothing but shame and despair."

The woman reached out, her fingers brushing against Vikram's face. The touch was cold, like the farmer's, but there was something more, something deeper. As her fingers traced the lines of his face,

Vikram felt a wave of emotion wash over him—fear, shame, guilt, and above all, a profound sense of loss. It was as if the woman's despair had become his own, a dark cloud that threatened to suffocate him.

"I trusted you," the woman continued, her voice trembling. "I believed you when you said you would protect me, that you would help me. But you lied, and now... now I have nothing."

The water rose higher, reaching Vikram's chest, the heat intensifying, the pain almost unbearable. The woman's touch lingered, a constant reminder of the suffering he had caused, the lives he had destroyed. And as she slowly disappeared beneath the surface, Vikram felt a piece of his soul being torn away, lost to the darkness of the river.

But there was no time to grieve, no time to reflect on the pain he had caused. The river pulled him forward, dragging him deeper into its depths, and the next soul emerged—a child, no more than ten years old, with hollow eyes and a face marked by hunger and despair.

Vikram's heart broke at the sight. The child was one of the many victims of his greed, a life cut short by the corruption that had plagued the very systems he had controlled. The child's eyes were wide with fear, and as he reached out to Vikram, his voice was barely a whisper.

"Why did you do it?" the child asked, his voice trembling with emotion. "Why did you take everything from us?"

The question was simple, but it cut deeper than any blade. Vikram had no answer, no defense, no excuse. The child's pain was his pain, the suffering of a life destroyed by his actions, and it was more than he could bear.

The child's hand touched Vikram's chest, and the pain intensified, a burning ache that spread through his entire body. It was as if the child's suffering was being transferred to him, a burden that he could not escape. The weight of the child's despair was overwhelming, a crushing force that left Vikram gasping for breath.

"I was hungry," the child continued, his voice barely audible. "I was so hungry, and you took everything... you took my life."

The child's voice faded, and as he disappeared

beneath the surface, Vikram felt a wave of guilt wash over him, a deep, soul-crushing regret that left him reeling. The water rose higher, now reaching his neck, the heat searing his flesh, the pain unbearable. But the river showed no mercy, and the current pulled him forward, dragging him deeper into the darkness.

As Vikram waded further into the river, more souls emerged, each one a victim of his corruption, each one a reminder of the pain he had caused. Their voices blended together in a haunting chorus, a symphony of suffering that echoed through the air, filling his mind with the weight of his sins.

A young mother, her face twisted in sorrow, spoke of the child she had lost, a life cut short by the lack of medical care that Vikram's embezzlement had made impossible. An old man, his eyes filled with bitterness, recounted the land that had been taken from him, his home destroyed by the greed of the powerful. A teacher, her voice trembling with anger, spoke of the school that had been closed, her students left with no future, no hope.

Each testimony was a blow to Vikram's soul,

a reminder of the lives he had destroyed, the suffering he had caused. The water burned, the pain seared, but it was nothing compared to the anguish that filled his heart, the overwhelming guilt that threatened to drown him.

The river seemed endless, a never-ending trial of torment and despair. With each step, the water rose higher, the current growing stronger, the voices of the damned echoing in his ears, a constant reminder of the suffering he had caused.

Vikram's strength began to wane, his body trembling with exhaustion, his mind fraying under the weight of his guilt. The river showed no mercy, and the souls continued to emerge, each one a new reminder of the pain he had inflicted, the lives he had ruined.

But as the water reached his chin, as the heat burned through his flesh, as the pain became almost too much to bear, Vikram felt something shift within him. It was a small, almost imperceptible change, a flicker of something deep within his soul.

For the first time, Vikram began to truly understand the full measure of his sins. The suffering he had caused was not just a consequence of his actions; it was a reflection of the darkness within him, the greed and corruption that had consumed his soul. The pain he felt was not just the punishment for his sins; it was a cleansing, a purging of the darkness that had tainted his soul for so long.

The realization was overwhelming, a flood of emotion that left Vikram reeling. The guilt, the shame, the regret—all of it surged through him, a torrent of feeling that threatened to drown him. But there was also something else, something deeper, something that had been buried beneath the layers of greed and corruption for so long.

It was a flicker of hope, a glimmer of light in the darkness.

Vikram had spent his life chasing after wealth and power, believing that they would bring him happiness, fulfillment, and security. But now, faced with the full measure of his sins, he saw the truth for what it was—an endless, insatiable hunger that had brought nothing but pain and suffering to himself and others.

The river had shown him the true cost of his

actions, the lives he had destroyed, the pain he had caused. But it had also given him a chance to atone, to face the consequences of his sins and begin the long, difficult journey toward redemption.

As the water reached his mouth, as the heat burned through his flesh, as the pain became almost too much to bear, Vikram made a decision. He would not run from the river, would not shy away from the suffering that awaited him. He would face it head-on, endure the pain, and accept the full measure of his sins.

And so, with a deep breath, Vikram took another step forward.

The water closed over his head, the heat searing through his flesh, the pain overwhelming. But Vikram did not struggle, did not fight. He let the river take him, let it pull him under, let it cleanse his soul of the darkness that had consumed him for so long.

The voices of the damned echoed in his ears, a haunting chorus of suffering and despair. The weight of his guilt pressed down on him, the pain of his sins searing through his soul. But Vikram did not resist. He accepted the suffering, embraced it, let it wash over him like a cleansing fire.

The river pulled him deeper into its depths, the darkness closing in around him, the voices of the damned fading into the distance. The pain was unbearable, the heat searing, but Vikram endured it, knowing that it was the price he had to pay, the burden he had to bear.

And as the darkness closed in, as the pain became almost too much to bear, Vikram felt something shift within him once more. The flicker of hope, the glimmer of light, grew stronger, brighter, a beacon in the darkness, guiding him forward.

Vikram had spent his life chasing after wealth and power, believing that they would bring him happiness. But now, faced with the full measure of his sins, he understood the true cost of his actions, the lives he had destroyed, the pain he had caused.

The river had shown him the way, had forced him to confront the suffering he had inflicted, the darkness within his soul. But it had also given him a chance, a chance to atone, to begin the long, difficult journey toward redemption.

As Vikram waded deeper into the river, as the pain seared through his flesh, as the darkness closed in around him, he knew that his journey was far from over. The road ahead was long and difficult, fraught with suffering and pain. But he was ready to face it, ready to endure whatever trials awaited him, knowing that it was the only way to cleanse his soul, to find redemption.

And so, with a heart filled with guilt and a soul burdened with the weight of his sins, Vikram Singh continued his journey through the River of Sins, knowing that the road ahead would be difficult, but determined to face whatever trials awaited him, knowing that it was the only way to atone for his sins and find redemption.

## Chapter 6

# The Forest of Thorns

Vikram Singh's journey through Naraka had already been filled with unimaginable torment. The scorching pain of the Vaitarna River had forced him to confront the numerous wrongs he had committed in his life. The agony of reliving the suffering he had caused, feeling the despair and hopelessness of those he had wronged, had been overwhelming. Yet, despite the pain, Vikram pressed on, driven by a faint hope that perhaps, somewhere along this dark path, there might be a chance for redemption.

But as the river's waters receded and Vikram stumbled onto solid ground, he found no respite. The air around him was thick with a cold, oppressive fog that seemed to seep into his very bones. The landscape before him was obscured, shrouded in darkness and shadow, but as he squinted through the gloom, he could make out the twisted, gnarled shapes of trees rising from the earth like skeletal fingers clawing at the sky.

This was the Forest of Thorns.

The forest loomed before him, a dense, impenetrable maze of twisted branches and sharp thorns. The trees were ancient, their bark dark and cracked, their limbs contorted as if in silent agony. The ground beneath them was covered in a thick carpet of decaying leaves and brambles, the thorns glistening with menace. The air was filled with the scent of decay, a pungent odor that clung to Vikram's senses and made him uneasy.

This was a place of reckoning, a manifestation of the lies, deceit, and betrayal that had characterized Vikram's life. Every thorn, every twisted branch, every gnarled root represented the tangled web of corruption he had woven, the countless false promises he had made, the betrayals he had committed in his relentless pursuit of power and wealth. The forest was a reflection of his soul, a dark, twisted mirror that showed him the true cost of the choices he had made.

Vikram hesitated at the edge of the forest, his heart pounding with dread. The pain of the river was still fresh in his mind, the memory of the souls he had wronged, their voices haunting him. And now, faced with the Forest of Thorns, he felt a deep, gnawing fear in the pit of his stomach. But he knew that there was no turning back, no escape from the path he had chosen. The only way forward was through the forest, to confront the lies and deceit that had defined his life, and to face the pain that awaited him within.

With a deep breath, Vikram took his first step into the forest.

The moment his foot touched the ground, he felt the sharp sting of a thorn pricking his skin. He winced but forced himself to keep moving, knowing that the pain was inevitable, that it was a part of the reckoning he deserved. The thorns tore at his clothes, ripping through the fabric, leaving his skin exposed to the biting cold and the sharp, unforgiving barbs that covered the ground.

Each step was a struggle, the dense undergrowth making it difficult to move, the thorns scratching at his skin, leaving marks in their wake. The pain was sharp, intense, but it was more than just physical.

With each thorn that pricked his skin, Vikram felt a deep, searing ache in his soul, as if the lies and betrayals he had committed in life were being exposed, one by one, each one leaving a raw, open wound.

The forest was silent, save for the rustle of leaves and the creak of branches swaying in the cold, stagnant air. But the silence was not comforting; it was oppressive, a heavy, suffocating weight that pressed down on Vikram, making it difficult to breathe. He felt as though he was being watched, as though the trees themselves were alive, their twisted branches reaching out to ensnare him, to drag him down into the darkness.

As he pushed deeper into the forest, the thorns grew thicker, more numerous, their barbs longer and sharper. The pain intensified, each step sending waves of discomfort through his body, the thorns scratching at his skin, leaving deep marks. But it was not just the physical pain that tormented him; it was the memories that the forest dredged up, the lies and deceit that he had tried so hard to forget, now brought to the surface, raw and painful.

With every thorn that pricked his skin, a memory rose to the forefront of his mind—a bribe accepted, a promise broken, a betrayal committed. The faces of those he had wronged flashed before his eyes, their expressions of pain and betrayal seared into his memory. The forest seemed to feed on his guilt, amplifying his torment, forcing him to confront the full extent of his misdeeds.

At times, the thorns seemed to take on a life of their own, the barbs twisting and coiling around his limbs, tightening like the shackles of his own deceit. They pulled at him, dragging him down, scratching at his skin, as if they were trying to pull him deeper into the darkness, to entangle him in the web of lies he had spun in life. Vikram struggled against them, but his strength was waning, the relentless pain sapping his will to fight.

The deeper he ventured into the forest, the more it seemed to close in around him, the trees pressing closer together, their twisted branches forming a dense canopy that blocked out the light. The air grew colder, the darkness more oppressive, and the thorns more numerous, their barbs digging deeper into his skin, leaving trails of discomfort that etched themselves into his mind.

But the worst of it was the isolation. The forest was a place of solitude, a prison of thorns that cut him off from the rest of the world, leaving him alone with his pain and his guilt. The silence was deafening, the only sounds his own labored breathing and the rustle of leaves beneath his feet. There was no escape from the memories that haunted him, no distraction from the pain that gnawed at his flesh and soul.

At times, the silence was broken by whispers—soft, barely audible voices that seemed to come from the very trees themselves. The whispers were filled with accusation, their words dripping with condemnation, reminding him of the lies he had told, the people he had betrayed, the lives he had altered. The voices grew louder as he pushed deeper into the forest, a chorus of accusation and judgment that echoed in his mind, driving him to the brink of despair.

"You deceived them, Vikram Singh," a voice murmured, the words like a cold wind against his ears. "You deceived and abandoned them, and now, you must face the consequences."

The thorny branches seemed to lash out at him, scratching his skin with renewed intensity, as if the forest itself was responding to his thoughts. Vikram flinched at the discomfort, but there was no one to hear his cries, no one to offer comfort or solace. He was alone, trapped in a prison of his own making, forced to confront the full extent of his corruption and deceit.

Another step, and a thorn scraped against his leg, the sensation sharp and unrelenting. He stumbled, falling to his knees, his hands sinking into the cold, damp earth. The thorns seemed to tighten around his arms, pulling him down, dragging him deeper into the undergrowth. He struggled to rise, but the discomfort was too much, the weight of his guilt too heavy. He felt as though he was being smothered by the forest, each thorn a reminder of the lies he had told, the people he had betrayed.

The faces of those he had wronged haunted him, their eyes filled with disappointment and hurt, their voices accusing him of the suffering he had caused. The weight of their grief pressed down on him, overwhelming him. He wanted to apologize, to seek forgiveness, but the words caught in his throat, trapped by the enormity of his guilt.

As Vikram moved deeper into the forest, the oppressive silence and the unrelenting thorns continued to torment him. The forest was not just a physical challenge; it was a journey through the darkest parts of his soul, forcing him to confront every lie, every betrayal, every moment of corruption that had led him to this place. The thorns that pricked and scratched his skin were reminders of the harm he had done, and the isolation he felt was a reflection of the isolation he had created in his own life, by pushing others away with his deceit.

But despite the discomfort, despite the isolation, Vikram knew he had to keep moving. The forest was a trial, a punishment for the lies and deceit that had defined his life. To give up, to surrender to the pain, would be to admit defeat, to accept that he was beyond redemption.

With great effort, Vikram pushed himself to his feet once more. The thorns scratched at his skin as he forced his way through the dense undergrowth, the branches clawing at him as if trying to hold him back. The discomfort was sharp, the isolation suffocating, but he pressed on, determined to face whatever lay ahead.

As he ventured deeper into the Forest of Thorns, Vikram began to understand the true nature of his punishment. The forest was not merely a place of pain and suffering; it was a mirror, reflecting the choices he had made in life, the lies he had told, the people he had hurt. Each thorn, each whisper, each moment of isolation was a reminder of the consequences of his actions, the price he had paid for his pursuit of power and wealth.

And yet, despite the harshness of the forest, Vikram began to sense something else as well—a glimmer of hope, a faint possibility of redemption. The forest was punishing him, yes, but it was also forcing him to confront his own soul, to acknowledge the harm he had done, and to seek a way to make amends. The journey through the Forest of Thorns was painful, but it was also a necessary step on the path to redemption.

Vikram continued to push forward, each step bringing new challenges, new moments of discomfort, but also new insights. The forest was unforgiving, but it was also transformative, forcing him to look inward, to confront the darkness within himself, and to seek a way to move beyond it.

The journey through the Forest of Thorns was far from over, and Vikram knew that the path ahead would be difficult. But he also knew that it was a path he had to walk, a journey he had to undertake if he was ever to find redemption. The thorns would continue to prick and scratch, the whispers would continue to haunt him, but Vikram was determined to press on, to face the consequences of his actions, and to seek a way to make things right.

And so, with the weight of his guilt heavy on his shoulders, but a newfound determination in his heart, Vikram Singh continued his journey through the Forest of Thorns, knowing that the path ahead would be difficult, but that it was a path he had to walk, a journey he had to complete if he was ever to find redemption.

## *Chapter 7*

# The Trial of Redemption

Vikram Singh had been through torment unimaginable. He had faced the searing heat of the Vaitarna River, reliving the agony of those he had wronged, and endured the suffocating isolation of the Forest of Thorns, each step a reminder of the tangled web of deceit he had woven in his life. The journey had left him battered, his soul laid bare to the truth of his actions. The pain, both physical and emotional, had been overwhelming, but even in the depths of despair, a flicker of hope had begun to grow within him. The hope that perhaps, despite all he had done, redemption might still be within his grasp.

But redemption was not something easily earned. The road ahead was fraught with trials, each more grueling than the last, requiring not only a deep transformation of his soul but also a genuine, heartfelt repentance for the harm he had caused.

Vikram knew that this would be the most difficult challenge of his life—or rather, his afterlife—but it was a challenge he had to face if he were ever to find peace.

As he emerged from the Forest of Thorns, Vikram found himself standing at the edge of a vast, barren plain. The ground was cracked and dry, the air heavy with the weight of anticipation. In the distance, he could see a faint glow, a soft light that seemed to beckon him forward. It was different from the harsh, punishing landscapes he had traversed so far—there was a warmth to it, a sense of possibility.

Vikram took a deep breath and began to walk toward the light. The ground beneath his feet was rough, the path uneven, but the light gave him a sense of purpose, guiding him toward what he hoped would be the beginning of his redemption. As he walked, the light grew brighter, and he could make out the outline of a grand structure ahead—a temple, ancient and majestic, its walls etched with intricate carvings that seemed to tell stories of long-forgotten times.

The closer Vikram got to the temple, the more he

felt the weight of his journey lifting, as if the very act of approaching this sacred place was purging his soul of the darkness that had consumed it for so long. The air around him grew warmer, the light more inviting, and for the first time in what felt like an eternity, Vikram allowed himself to hope.

As he reached the steps of the temple, Vikram paused, taking in the grandeur of the structure before him. The temple was unlike anything he had ever seen—its walls were adorned with scenes of great battles, acts of heroism, and moments of profound peace. But there were also depictions of suffering, of souls lost in the darkness, struggling to find their way back to the light. It was a place of duality, representing both the potential for greatness and the consequences of falling into despair.

Vikram ascended the steps, each one feeling like a step closer to the possibility of redemption. At the top of the stairs, he found himself standing before a massive door, its surface carved with symbols and runes that seemed to pulse with a life of their own. The door was slightly ajar, and beyond it, Vikram could see a soft, golden light spilling out, bathing the entrance in a warm, inviting glow.

Taking a deep breath, Vikram pushed the door open and stepped inside.

The interior of the temple was vast, its walls lined with towering columns that reached up to a ceiling that seemed to stretch into infinity. The light that filled the space was soft and golden, casting a warm glow over everything it touched. In the center of the room stood a grand altar, upon which rested a simple, unadorned book. The book was ancient, its pages yellowed with age, but there was a power to it, a sense that it held within its pages the wisdom of the ages.

Vikram approached the altar, his footsteps echoing in the silence of the temple. As he reached the book, he hesitated for a moment, unsure of what to do next. But then, as if guided by an unseen force, he reached out and opened the book.

The pages were filled with words written in a language Vikram did not recognize, but as he looked closer, the words began to shift and change, transforming into a language he could understand.

The book was a guide, a manual of sorts, outlining the steps he would need to take to achieve redemption. But it was not a simple list of tasks; it was a series of trials, each one designed to test the very core of his being, to strip away the layers of corruption and deceit that had defined his life, and to reveal the true nature of his soul.

Vikram knew that these trials would be grueling, requiring not only physical endurance but also a deep, spiritual transformation. He would need to confront the darkest parts of himself, to seek forgiveness from those he had wronged, and to perform acts of selflessness and humility that would begin to atone for the harm he had caused. But he was ready. For the first time in his life—or afterlife—he was truly ready to face the consequences of his actions and to seek redemption with all his heart.

As he read through the pages of the book, the first trial began to take shape in his mind. It was a trial of humility, a test designed to strip away the arrogance and pride that had defined his life. Vikram would need to confront the souls of those he had wronged, to seek their forgiveness, and to offer them whatever he could to make amends. It was a daunting task, but one that he knew was necessary if he were ever to find peace.

The temple began to fade from around him, and Vikram found himself standing in a familiar place—the office where he had once held power, where he had made decisions that had affected the lives of countless people. But the office was not as he remembered it. It was dark and cold, the walls covered in shadows, the air heavy with the weight of his past actions.

Before him stood a figure, its form indistinct but familiar. As the figure stepped into the light, Vikram's heart sank—it was the spirit of a man he had once betrayed, a man who had come to him for help, only to be turned away. The man's face was etched with pain and sorrow, his eyes filled with the weight of the suffering Vikram had caused.

Vikram knew what he had to do. He stepped forward, his heart heavy with guilt, and bowed his head before the man. "I am sorry," he said, his voice trembling with emotion. "I betrayed you, and for that, I ask for your forgiveness."

The man's eyes bore into Vikram's, and for a moment, there was silence. Then, slowly, the man reached out and placed a hand on Vikram's shoulder. "I forgive you," he said, his voice soft but firm. "But forgiveness is not enough. You must make amends for the harm you have caused. You must help those you have wronged."

Vikram nodded, tears filling his eyes. He knew that the man was right. Forgiveness was not enough—he needed to take action, to perform acts of selflessness and humility that would begin to atone for his sins.

As the man's spirit faded, Vikram found himself back in the temple, standing before the altar once more. The book was still open, its pages filled with the next steps of his journey. The first trial had been completed, but there were many more to come.

The next trial was one of selflessness. Vikram would need to seek out those he had wronged and offer them whatever help he could, without expecting anything in return. It was a test of his willingness to put others before himself, to act not out of a desire for power or wealth, but out of a genuine desire to make things right.

The scene around him shifted once more, and Vikram found himself standing in a village he had once visited during his time in power. The village was small and poor, its people struggling to survive. Vikram had promised them help, but instead, he had taken the funds meant for them and used them for his own gain.

As he walked through the village, Vikram could feel the weight of his past actions pressing down on him. The people here had suffered because of his greed, and now it was time to make amends. He approached a group of villagers, their faces gaunt and weary, their eyes filled with suspicion and distrust.

"I am here to help," Vikram said, his voice filled with sincerity. "I know I have wronged you in the past, but I want to make things right. Please, let me help you."

The villagers looked at him with skepticism, but one by one, they began to step forward, telling him of their needs, their struggles, and their hopes for a better future. Vikram listened to each of them, his heart heavy with guilt, and promised to do whatever he could to help.

He spent days in the village, working alongside the villagers, helping to rebuild their homes, providing them with the resources they needed, and ensuring that the promises he made were kept. It was grueling work, but with each act of selflessness, Vikram felt a small piece of the burden lift from his soul.

As he worked, Vikram began to see the villagers not as mere victims of his greed, but as people with hopes, dreams, and aspirations of their own. He realized that his actions had not only caused them physical harm but had also taken away their sense of dignity and hope. By helping them, he was not just making amends for his past actions, but also helping to restore their sense of self-worth.

The trial of selflessness was not just about performing acts of charity; it was about learning to see others as equals, as individuals with their own struggles and desires. It was about learning to put the needs of others before his own, and to act not out of a desire for recognition or reward, but out of a genuine desire to help.

As the days passed, Vikram felt a change within himself. The arrogance and pride that had once defined him began to fade, replaced by a sense of humility and empathy. He began to understand that true power did not come from wealth or status, but from the ability to make a positive difference in the lives of others.

When his work in the village was complete, Vikram returned to the temple. The book was still open on the altar, its pages filled with the next steps of his journey. The trial of selflessness had been completed, but there were still more trials to come.

The next trial was one of forgiveness. Vikram would need to seek out those who had wronged him in life and offer them his forgiveness, without holding on to any resentment or anger. It was a test of his ability to let go of the past, to release the grudges he had held onto, and to find peace within himself.

The scene around him shifted once more, and Vikram found himself standing in front of a grand mansion—the home of a man who had once been his greatest rival. The man had betrayed Vikram, spreading lies and rumors that had damaged his reputation and caused him great harm. In life, Vikram had harbored a deep hatred for this man, vowing to take revenge, but now, in the afterlife, he knew that he had to let go of that anger if he were ever to find peace.

As he approached the mansion, Vikram felt a surge of anger rise within him, the old wounds reopening. But he knew that this was a test, a trial that he had to pass if he were to achieve redemption. He took a deep breath and knocked on the door.

The man who answered the door was older than Vikram remembered, his face lined with age and regret. The man's eyes widened in shock as he saw Vikram standing before him, but before he could speak, Vikram raised a hand.

"I have come to forgive you," Vikram said, his voice calm and steady. "You wronged me in life, but I hold no grudge against you. I have let go of my anger, and I ask that you do the same."

The man's expression softened, and tears filled his eyes. "I am sorry, Vikram," he said, his voice trembling with emotion. "I have lived with the guilt of what I did to you for many years. I was wrong, and I hope that you can find it in your heart to forgive me."

"I already have," Vikram replied, feeling a sense of peace wash over him. "What's done is done. We cannot change the past, but we can choose how we move forward. I forgive you, and I hope you can forgive yourself."

The man nodded, a look of relief crossing his face. "Thank you, Vikram," he said. "I will never forget this act of kindness."

As the man's spirit faded, Vikram felt a weight lift from his shoulders. The trial of forgiveness had been completed, and with it, another piece of the darkness within him had been dispelled. He knew that there were still more trials to come, but with each one, he felt himself growing stronger, more at peace with himself and the choices he had made.

When he returned to the temple, the book on the altar was still open, its pages now filled with the final steps of his journey. The last trial was the most difficult of all—a trial of acceptance. Vikram would need to accept the full weight of his actions, to fully acknowledge the harm he had caused, and to take responsibility for it without seeking to justify or excuse his behavior.

The scene around him shifted once more, and Vikram found himself standing in a courtroom—a place where, in life, he had often wielded his power to manipulate outcomes in his favor. But this time, he was not the one in control. He was the one on trial, his every action laid bare for judgment.

The judge, a figure of great authority, stood before him, his expression stern but fair. "Vikram Singh," the judge intoned, his voice echoing through the courtroom. "You are here to face the consequences of your actions. Do you accept responsibility for the harm you have caused?"

Vikram felt a lump rise in his throat, but he knew that this was the moment of truth. He could no longer hide behind excuses or justifications. He had to face the full weight of his actions, to accept responsibility for the lives he had harmed.

"Yes," Vikram replied, his voice steady. "I accept full responsibility for my actions. I caused harm to many people, and I take responsibility for the pain and suffering I caused."

The judge nodded, his expression softening. "Acceptance is the first step toward redemption, Vikram Singh," he said. "But acceptance alone is not enough. You must also seek to make amends, to do whatever you can to repair the damage you have done."

Vikram nodded, a sense of determination filling him. "I will do whatever it takes," he said. "I will spend the rest of my existence making amends for the harm I have caused."

The judge's expression softened further, and he gave a small nod of approval. "Very well," he said. "Your journey toward redemption is far from over, but you have taken the first steps. Continue on this path, and you may yet find the peace you seek."

As the scene faded, Vikram found himself back in the temple, standing before the altar. The book was still open, but its pages were now blank, as if to signify that the next steps of his journey were for him to write. The trials he had faced had been grueling, but they had also been transformative, each one stripping away the layers of corruption and deceit that had defined his life, and revealing the true nature of his soul.

Vikram knew that his journey was far from over. The road ahead would be difficult, filled with challenges and trials that would test his resolve and his commitment to redemption. But he was ready. For the first time in his existence, he felt a sense of purpose, a sense that he was on the path to becoming the person he was meant to be.

As he left the temple, Vikram looked back at the grand structure one last time, feeling a deep sense of gratitude for the trials he had faced within its walls. The temple had been a place of transformation, a place where he had begun the process of redeeming his soul.

With a renewed sense of determination, Vikram set out on the next stage of his journey, knowing that the path ahead would be long and difficult, but also knowing that he was no longer alone. The trials he had faced had brought him closer to the light, and he knew that, with each step he took, he was one step closer to achieving the redemption he so desperately sought.

### *Chapter 8*

# The Light of Satya

Vikram Singh had come a long way in his journey through Naraka. The trials of redemption had tested him in ways he had never imagined, stripping away the layers of deceit, arrogance, and corruption that had defined his life. He had faced the souls he had wronged, sought their forgiveness, and performed acts of selflessness and humility that began to atone for the harm he had caused. Each trial had been a step closer to the light, a step closer to becoming the person he was meant to be.

Now, as he emerged from the temple where he had faced these trials, Vikram felt a profound sense of change within himself. The burden of his past sins was still there, but it was lighter, no longer crushing him under its weight. He had begun to understand the true nature of redemption—not as a destination, but as a journey, a continuous process of transformation and growth.

But the journey was not yet over. As Vikram looked ahead, he saw a path bathed in a soft, radiant light. It was unlike anything he had encountered in Naraka so far—pure, warm, and inviting. The light seemed to call out to him, drawing him forward with a promise of truth and clarity.

This was the Light of Satya, the embodiment of truth.

Vikram took a deep breath and began to walk toward the light. The path was smooth and even, a stark contrast to the rough, treacherous terrain he had traversed before. As he walked, the light grew brighter, enveloping him in its warmth. It was a comforting presence, soothing the wounds that the trials of redemption had left on his soul.

As he moved closer to the source of the light, Vikram noticed that the landscape around him had changed. The barren, desolate plains of Naraka were gone, replaced by a lush, verdant landscape. The air was filled with the scent of blooming flowers, and the sound of birdsong filled his ears. It was as if he had entered a different realm entirely—a realm of peace and serenity.

But even in this tranquil place, Vikram knew that he was not yet free of the consequences of his actions. The Light of Satya was not merely a place of rest; it was a place of reflection, a place where he would be asked to confront the truth of his life and the lessons he had learned along the way.

As he continued down the path, Vikram saw a figure standing at the end of the road. The figure was bathed in the radiant light, its features indistinct, but there was an undeniable sense of power and wisdom emanating from it. Vikram knew instinctively that this was the guardian of the Light of Satya, the one who would guide him through this final stage of his journey.

When Vikram reached the figure, he bowed his head in respect, acknowledging the presence of the guardian. The figure inclined its head in return, and then spoke, its voice calm and measured, yet filled with an authority that commanded attention.

"Vikram Singh," the guardian said, "you have come far in your journey. You have faced the trials of redemption and have begun to atone for the sins of your past. But before you can move forward, you must confront the truth of your life and the lessons you have learned. Only then can you fully understand the path you must take."

Vikram nodded, his heart heavy with anticipation. He knew that this would not be an easy task. The truth was often difficult to face, especially for someone who had spent so much of his life hiding from it, manipulating it to suit his own ends. But he also knew that this was a necessary step, one that would allow him to fully embrace the transformation he had undergone.

The guardian gestured for Vikram to follow, and together they walked deeper into the light. As they did, the light around them grew even brighter, until it was almost blinding. But Vikram did not shy away from it. He welcomed the light, knowing that it would illuminate the darkest corners of his soul, revealing the truth that he had long sought to avoid.

After what felt like an eternity, the guardian stopped and turned to face Vikram. "The Light of Satya reveals all," the guardian said. "It will show you the truth of your life, the consequences of your actions, and the lessons you were meant to learn.

But it will also offer you a vision—a glimpse of what your life could have been had you chosen the path of honesty and service. Are you ready to face this truth?"

Vikram hesitated for a moment, fear and uncertainty gnawing at the edges of his resolve. But then he remembered the journey he had already undertaken, the trials he had faced, and the transformation he had begun to experience. He had come too far to turn back now.

"I am ready," Vikram said, his voice steady.

The guardian nodded, and with a wave of its hand, the light around them intensified, surrounding Vikram in a warm, radiant glow. The light was all-encompassing, filling his vision, his mind, his very soul. And then, slowly, the light began to take shape, forming images and scenes that played out before him like a film.

The first image was of his early life, the time before he had fallen into the trap of corruption and greed. He saw himself as a young man, full of ambition and dreams, eager to make a difference in the world. He had entered public service with the noble intention of helping others, of using his position to bring about positive change. But somewhere along the way, that noble purpose had been lost.

The scene shifted, showing Vikram in his prime, a powerful bureaucrat with influence and wealth. But instead of using that power for the greater good, he had used it to enrich himself, to manipulate others for his own gain. He saw himself making deals in dark corners, accepting bribes, turning a blind eye to the suffering of those he was meant to serve. The faces of the people he had wronged flashed before him—farmers driven to despair, families torn apart, lives ruined by his actions.

The pain of these memories was sharp, a reminder of the harm he had caused. But the Light of Satya did not allow him to turn away. It forced him to confront these truths, to acknowledge the impact of his choices, and to feel the full weight of his actions.

And then, just as the pain became almost too much to bear, the light shifted again, showing Vikram a different vision—a vision of what his life could have been.

In this vision, Vikram saw himself as the man he could have been, had he chosen the path of honesty and service. He saw a life filled with purpose and fulfillment, a life where he used his power and influence to uplift others, to bring about positive change in the world. He saw himself working tirelessly to improve the lives of those he served, advocating for policies that benefited the poor and marginalized, fighting against corruption and injustice.

In this alternate life, Vikram was respected and loved by those he served. He was a beacon of hope, a symbol of what a public servant could and should be. The satisfaction and contentment he felt in this life were palpable, a stark contrast to the emptiness and regret that had filled his real life.

As the vision played out before him, Vikram felt a deep sense of sorrow and regret. He realized how different his life could have been if he had chosen the path of truth, if he had remained true to his original purpose. But he also felt a sense of clarity—a recognition of the lessons he was meant to learn.

The vision continued, showing Vikram not only the impact he could have had on the lives of others but also the impact on his own soul. In this alternate life, he was at peace with himself, free from the guilt and shame that had plagued him in his real life. He had found true fulfillment, not in wealth or power, but in the knowledge that he had made a positive difference in the world.

The contrast between the two lives was stark and undeniable. The life Vikram had lived—a life of deceit, corruption, and personal gain—had brought him nothing but pain and regret. The life he could have lived—a life of honesty, service, and truth—would have brought him peace, fulfillment, and a lasting legacy.

As the vision faded, Vikram found himself once again standing before the guardian in the radiant light. The images he had seen continued to play in his mind, the lessons they conveyed sinking deep into his soul.

"The Light of Satya has shown you the truth," the guardian said, its voice gentle but firm. "It has revealed to you the consequences of your actions and the life you could have had if you had chosen the path of truth. What have you learned from this?"

Vikram took a deep breath, his mind racing as he tried to process everything he had seen. "I have learned that truth is the foundation of a meaningful life," he said, his voice filled with conviction. "I see now that the choices I made were driven by greed and a desire for power, but they brought me nothing but emptiness and pain. The life I could have had—one of honesty and service—would have brought me true fulfillment and peace."

The guardian nodded, as if satisfied with Vikram's answer. "You have learned an important lesson, Vikram Singh," it said. "Truth is the light that guides us, the force that gives our lives meaning. Without it, we are lost, wandering in the darkness of our own making. But with it, we can find our way, no matter how far we have strayed from the path."

Vikram felt a sense of relief wash over him. The burden of his past sins was still there, but it was no longer crushing him. The Light of Satya had shown him the way forward, had given him the clarity he needed to continue his journey toward redemption.

But the guardian was not finished. "There is one more thing you must understand," it said. "The life you could have had is not lost to you. You still have the power to choose the path of truth, to live a life of honesty and service. But it will require great effort, and it will not be easy. Are you willing to commit to this path, knowing the challenges that lie ahead?"

Vikram did not hesitate. "Yes," he said, his voice steady and resolute. "I am willing to commit to the path of truth, no matter how difficult it may be. I have seen what my life could have been, and I know that it is the life I want to live."

The guardian smiled, a warm, radiant smile that seemed to fill the entire space with light. "Then your journey is not over, Vikram Singh," it said. "You have taken the first steps toward redemption, but there is still much work to be done. The path of truth is not an easy one, but it is the only path that leads to true peace and fulfillment. Walk it with courage, and you will find the light that you seek."

With those words, the guardian began to fade, and the light around Vikram dimmed, returning him to the lush, verdant landscape where his journey had begun. But now, there was a difference. The path before him was clear, illuminated by the light of Satya, guiding him forward.

Vikram knew that the road ahead would be difficult. He would need to continue to atone for his past sins, to seek out those he had wronged, and to make amends wherever possible. He would need to live each day with honesty and integrity, to put the needs of others before his own, and to strive to make a positive difference in the world.

But he also knew that he was no longer alone. The Light of Satya was with him, guiding him, showing him the way forward. And with each step he took, he would move closer to the redemption he so desperately sought.

As Vikram set out on this new path, he felt a sense of peace and purpose that he had never known before. The trials of Naraka had tested him, had brought him to the brink of despair, but they had also transformed him, showing him the true nature of his soul and the life he was meant to live.

The journey was far from over, but for the first time, Vikram felt ready to face whatever challenges lay ahead. The Light of Satya had shown him the truth, and with that truth came the power to change, to become the person he was always meant to be.

And so, with the light of truth guiding his way, Vikram Singh continued his journey, knowing that the path ahead would be difficult, but also knowing that it was the only path that led to true peace and fulfillment.

The light of Satya was with him, and with each step he took, he moved closer to the redemption he sought, closer to the person he was meant to be.

## *Chapter 9*

# The Choice of Rebirth

Vikram Singh stood at the threshold of a new beginning. The Light of Satya had illuminated the path before him, revealing the truth of his past actions and the lessons he was meant to learn. The journey through Naraka had been grueling, each trial stripping away the layers of deceit, arrogance, and greed that had defined his life. He had been humbled, transformed, and now, as he stood on the brink of his next trial, he was offered a choice that would determine the course of his soul's future.

The lush, verdant landscape that had surrounded him after his encounter with the Light of Satya began to shift once more. The ground beneath his feet trembled, and the air around him shimmered with an ethereal glow. Vikram felt a sense of anticipation, a knowing that the next step in his journey would be unlike anything he had faced before.

As the landscape continued to change, Vikram

found himself standing before a grand archway, its surface carved with intricate designs that seemed to pulse with a living energy. Beyond the archway, a new realm awaited—a place where the concept of time and space was fluid, where the boundaries between life, death, and rebirth were blurred. This was the realm of choice, the place where souls were given the opportunity to decide their own fate.

Standing beside the archway was a figure of immense stature, radiating a presence that was both comforting and awe-inspiring. This was the guide of the realm, the keeper of the choices that souls must make before they could move forward on their journey. The figure's face was serene, its eyes filled with a deep wisdom that transcended time.

"Vikram Singh," the guide said, its voice resonating with a gentle authority, "you have come far in your journey. You have faced the trials of Naraka and the Light of Satya. You have confronted the truth of your life and learned the lessons that were meant to guide you. But your journey is not yet complete. Before you can move forward, you must make a choice—a choice that will determine the course of your soul's future."

Vikram felt a weight settle in his chest, the enormity of the moment pressing down on him. This was the moment of decision, the moment where he would determine the next chapter of his existence. He knew that this choice was not one to be made lightly, for it would shape the very essence of his soul.

The guide extended a hand toward the archway, and as it did, the space beyond the archway began to shift and shimmer, revealing a series of images—visions of lives yet to be lived, paths yet to be taken. Each vision was a glimpse into the possibilities that lay before Vikram, each one a different way in which he could continue his journey.

"Before you is the choice of rebirth," the guide said, its voice filled with a solemn reverence. "Rebirth is a sacred opportunity, a chance for the soul to return to the world of the living and to pursue a life of virtue and righteousness. In Hinduism, the cycle of birth, death, and rebirth is known as samsara, and it is through this cycle that the soul is given the opportunity to rectify its past mistakes and to grow in wisdom and understanding."

The guide paused, allowing Vikram to take in the significance of the words. "You have the choice to be reborn," the guide continued. "But this rebirth will not be as the powerful bureaucrat you once were. Instead, you will return to earth as a humble servant of the people, with the knowledge of your past life and the lessons you have learned. It will be a life of simplicity, but it will also be a life of great purpose—a life dedicated to the service of others and the pursuit of truth."

As the guide spoke, the images beyond the archway began to solidify, forming a clear vision of the life that Vikram could choose. He saw himself reborn as a humble man, living in a small village, far removed from the centers of power and wealth that had once defined his existence. In this life, he was a teacher, a healer, a guide to those who sought wisdom and understanding. He lived a simple life, but it was a life filled with meaning—a life where he used his knowledge and experience to help others, to lift them up, and to guide them on their own journeys.

Vikram watched the vision unfold before him, feeling a deep sense of connection to this new life. He saw the faces of the people he would serve—men, women, and children who came to him seeking guidance, comfort, and healing. He saw himself working tirelessly to improve their lives, teaching them the values of honesty, compassion, and humility. He saw the joy in their faces when they found the strength to overcome their challenges, the peace they felt when they embraced the truth of their own lives.

But this vision also came with challenges. Vikram saw the hardships he would face—the poverty, the illness, the struggles of those he would serve. He saw the moments of doubt and despair, the times when he would question whether he was making a difference, whether he was truly on the right path. He saw the sacrifices he would have to make, the personal desires he would have to set aside in order to fulfill his duty to others.

Yet, despite these challenges, Vikram felt a deep sense of fulfillment in this life—a sense that he was finally living in alignment with the values and principles he had come to understand through his journey in Naraka. It was a life of humility and service, but it was also a life of profound meaning and purpose.

The guide allowed Vikram to take in the vision for a moment longer before speaking again. "This is one possible path," the guide said. "But there are others. The choice of rebirth is yours to make, and you may choose to return to a different life, or even to continue on your current path without the need for rebirth. But know this: the choices you make will shape the course of your soul's journey, and they will determine whether you continue to grow in wisdom and understanding, or whether you fall back into the patterns of your past."

Vikram felt a sense of trepidation as the guide spoke. The weight of the decision before him was immense, and he knew that the choice he made now would have far-reaching consequences. But he also knew that he had been given a rare and precious opportunity—a chance to correct the mistakes of his past and to live a life that was truly in service to others.

The guide gestured once more, and the vision of the humble life in the village began to fade, replaced by a new vision—a vision of a life lived in solitude and contemplation. In this life, Vikram saw himself as a monk, living in a remote ashram, far from the distractions of the world. He spent his days in meditation and study, seeking to deepen his understanding of the nature of existence and the path to liberation from samsara.

This life was one of simplicity and peace, but it was also a life of great discipline and sacrifice. Vikram saw himself dedicating his life to the pursuit of spiritual knowledge, renouncing all worldly attachments and desires. He saw the peace that came with this life, the deep sense of connection to the divine that he experienced in his moments of meditation and prayer.

But he also saw the challenges of this path—the loneliness, the isolation, the moments of doubt and uncertainty. He saw the sacrifices he would have to make, the relationships he would have to forgo, the worldly pleasures he would have to renounce in order to stay true to his spiritual path.

As he watched this vision unfold, Vikram felt a sense of resonance with this life as well. It was a life of deep spiritual fulfillment, a life where he could continue to grow in wisdom and understanding. But it was also a life that required great discipline and sacrifice, and he knew that it would not be an easy path to follow.

The guide allowed the vision to play out before it too began to fade, replaced by yet another vision—a vision of a life of power and influence. In this life, Vikram saw himself reborn as a leader, a figure of authority who wielded great influence over others. He was a man of wealth and power, respected and feared by those around him. But unlike his previous life as a bureaucrat, in this life he used his power for the greater good, to bring about positive change in the world.

He saw himself advocating for justice and equality, fighting against corruption and oppression, and using his influence to improve the lives of those who were less fortunate. He was a leader who commanded respect, but he was also a leader who understood the importance of humility and service. He used his wealth and power not for personal gain, but to uplift others and to create a more just and equitable society.

This vision was one of strength and purpose, but it was also a life filled with challenges. Vikram saw the pressures and responsibilities that came with power, the difficult decisions he would have to make, the enemies he would face, and the constant threat of falling back into the patterns of greed and corruption that had defined his previous life.

As the vision played out, Vikram felt a sense of conflict within himself. This life offered the opportunity to make a significant impact on the world, to use his skills and experience to bring about meaningful change. But it also carried the risk of repeating the mistakes of his past, of succumbing to the temptations of power and wealth.

The guide's voice broke through Vikram's thoughts, drawing his attention back to the present. "Each of these lives offers a different path," the guide said. "The life of service, the life of contemplation, the life of power—each has its own challenges and rewards. But the choice is yours to make. You must decide which path will allow your soul to grow in wisdom and understanding, and which will bring you closer to the truth."

Vikram stood in silence, his mind racing as he considered the choices before him. Each life offered a different way forward, each one a different opportunity to atone for his past and to pursue a life of virtue and righteousness. But he knew that the decision he made now would not only affect his own soul but also the lives of those he would encounter on his journey.

He thought back to the lessons he had learned in Naraka, the trials he had faced, and the truths he had come to understand. He remembered the faces of those he had wronged, the pain he had caused, and the deep sense of regret that had accompanied his journey. But he also remembered the glimmer of hope that had begun to grow within him, the sense of purpose that had driven him to seek redemption.

As he considered the lives before him, Vikram realized that each path offered him the opportunity to continue that journey of redemption. But each path also required a different kind of commitment, a different kind of sacrifice.

The life of service called to him with its promise of humility and purpose. It was a life where he could make a direct impact on the lives of others, where he could use his knowledge and experience to uplift those who were struggling and to guide them toward a better future. But it was also a life of hardship, where he would face challenges and sacrifices that would test his resolve.

The life of contemplation offered the promise of spiritual fulfillment and peace. It was a life where he could deepen his understanding of the nature of existence and work toward liberation from samsara. But it was also a life of solitude, where he would be removed from the world and the opportunity to directly impact the lives of others.

The life of power offered the opportunity to wield influence and bring about significant change in the world. It was a life where he could use his skills and experience to fight against injustice and oppression, to create a more just and equitable society. But it was also a life filled with challenges and temptations, where the risk of falling back into old patterns of greed and corruption was ever-present.

Vikram knew that there was no easy answer, no perfect choice. Each path had its own merits and its own challenges, and each one offered the opportunity for growth and redemption.

But as he stood before the archway, Vikram felt a deep sense of clarity settle over him. He realized that the choice he made did not have to be about choosing the easiest path or the one with the least risk. It was about choosing the path that resonated most deeply with the person he had become, the path that would allow him to continue his journey of redemption in a way that was true to his soul.

With this understanding, Vikram made his decision.

He turned to the guide, his voice steady and resolute. "I choose the life of service," he said. "I choose to return to the world as a humble servant of the people, with the knowledge of my past life and the lessons I have learned. I believe that this is the path that will allow me to make the greatest impact, to atone for my past mistakes, and to continue my journey toward redemption."

The guide smiled, a warm and approving smile that filled Vikram with a sense of peace. "You have chosen wisely, Vikram Singh," the guide said. "The life of service is a noble path, one that requires great humility and dedication. It will not be easy, but it will be filled with purpose and meaning. Through this life, you will have the opportunity to make a difference in the lives of others, to uplift those who are struggling, and to bring light to those who are lost in darkness."

As the guide spoke, the archway before Vikram began to glow with a radiant light, signaling that the path he had chosen was ready for him to walk. The visions of the other lives faded away, leaving only the image of the humble servant, the life that Vikram had chosen for his rebirth.

"Remember," the guide said, its voice filled with gentle wisdom, "the path of service is not about seeking recognition or reward. It is about putting the needs of others before your own, about acting with compassion, humility, and integrity. It is about living in alignment with the truth, the Satya, that you have come to understand. If you remain true to this path, you will find the redemption you seek."

Vikram nodded, his heart filled with determination. The path of service was not an easy one, but it was the path that resonated most deeply with the person he had become. He was ready to embrace this new life, to face the challenges it would bring, and to continue his journey of redemption with a renewed sense of purpose.

The guide stepped aside, allowing Vikram to approach the archway. The light within the archway grew brighter, enveloping him in its warmth as he prepared to take the final step.

"Are you ready?" the guide asked, its voice filled with quiet anticipation.

Vikram took a deep breath, his heart steady and calm. "Yes," he said. "I am ready."

With those words, Vikram stepped through the archway and into the light.

The light surrounded him, filling him with a sense of peace and clarity. He felt his soul being lifted, carried by the light as it transported him to his new life, the life of service that he had chosen. The memories of his past life, the lessons he had learned, and the truths he had come to understand all remained with him, guiding him as he prepared to begin this new chapter of his existence.

As the light carried him forward, Vikram felt a deep sense of gratitude—for the trials he had faced, for the lessons he had learned, and for the opportunity to continue his journey in a way that was true to his soul. He knew that the road ahead would be difficult, but he also knew that it was the right path, the path that would allow him to continue growing in wisdom and understanding.

And so, with a heart filled with purpose and a soul filled with light, Vikram Singh embraced his rebirth, ready to live a life of service, humility, and truth.

The journey of redemption was far from over, but with each step he took, he moved closer to the peace and fulfillment that he had sought for so long.

The light began to fade, and as it did, Vikram felt himself descending into the world of the living, the memories of his past life blending with the knowledge of his new purpose.

He was ready to begin again, to live a life dedicated to the greater good, to serve others with compassion and integrity.

The choice of rebirth had been made, and with it, Vikram Singh's journey toward redemption continued.

## *Chapter 10*

# The New Life

Vikram Singh's journey had brought him through the depths of Naraka, through the trials of redemption, and finally to the choice of rebirth. With the memories of his past life and the lessons he had learned still fresh in his mind, he stepped through the archway into the radiant light, ready to begin his new life as a humble servant of the people.

The light enveloped him, carrying him through the threshold of existence and into a new beginning. Vikram felt his consciousness fading, the details of his previous life slipping away, not lost, but gently stored in the recesses of his soul, waiting to guide him when the time was right. As the light dimmed, he felt himself descending, his spirit merging with a new body, ready to experience the world once more—but this time, with the wisdom he had earned through his trials.

**The First Steps**

Vikram was reborn into a modest family in a small village far from the centers of power and wealth that had once defined his existence. His new parents, Devendra and Kamala, were humble farmers who worked tirelessly to make ends meet. They lived in a simple, thatched-roof house surrounded by fields of rice and wheat, the air filled with the scent of earth and the sounds of nature.

From the moment he was born, it was clear that Vikram, now named Anant, was different. Even as a child, he displayed a quiet wisdom and an unusual sensitivity to the world around him. He was curious and eager to learn, but there was also a depth to his gaze that belied his years, as if he carried within him the experiences of many lifetimes.

Devendra and Kamala noticed these qualities in their son and nurtured them with care. They were simple people, but they valued education and instilled in Anant a love of learning from an early age. Despite their limited means, they made sacrifices to send him to the local school, where he quickly excelled in his studies. But it wasn't just academic achievement that set Anant apart—it was his deep sense of justice and his unwavering commitment to doing what was right.

As he grew, Anant found himself drawn to stories of great leaders and reformers, men and women who had dedicated their lives to serving others and fighting for justice. He devoured books about Mahatma Gandhi, B.R. Ambedkar, and other figures who had played pivotal roles in shaping India's history. These stories resonated deeply with him, igniting a fire in his soul and fueling his desire to make a difference in the world.

Yet, even as he dreamed of changing the world, Anant remained grounded in the values his parents had taught him. He saw the struggles of the farmers in his village, the challenges they faced in their daily lives, and he understood the importance of honesty, integrity, and hard work. These values became the foundation upon which he built his life, guiding his decisions and shaping his character.

**The Call to Service**

By the time Anant reached his teenage years, his path was becoming clear. He knew that his purpose in life was to serve others, to use his talents and knowledge to help those in need. But he also understood that this would not be an easy path. The world was filled with challenges and injustices, and he would need to be strong, resilient, and unwavering in his commitment to his values.

After completing his basic education in the village, Anant earned a scholarship to attend a prestigious university in the city. It was a momentous occasion for his family, a testament to the hard work and sacrifices they had made to support his education. But for Anant, it was also a stepping stone toward his larger goal—becoming a true servant of the people.

The transition from village life to the bustling city was not easy. The city was a place of contrasts, where extreme wealth and poverty existed side by side, where power and corruption often overshadowed honesty and integrity. Anant was exposed to a world that was far removed from the simple, honest life he had known, and it tested his resolve in ways he had never imagined.

But instead of being overwhelmed, Anant saw the city as a microcosm of the challenges facing the country. He saw the need for reform, for leaders who would stand up against corruption and fight for the rights of the marginalized. He saw the struggles of the poor, the injustices faced by the disadvantaged, and the rampant inequality that plagued society. And he knew that he had to do something about it.

During his time at the university, Anant became deeply involved in student activism. He joined organizations dedicated to social justice, human rights, and environmental sustainability. He participated in protests, organized campaigns, and worked tirelessly to raise awareness about the issues that mattered most to him. His passion for justice and his commitment to service quickly earned him the respect of his peers and professors alike.

But Anant's activism was not just about raising his voice—it was about making a tangible difference. He volunteered with local NGOs, working directly with communities affected by poverty and discrimination. He helped organize health camps, educational programs, and legal aid clinics, providing support to those who needed it most.

Through these experiences, he gained a deeper understanding of the systemic issues that plagued society, and he became even more determined to address them.

The Lessons of the Past

Throughout his journey, the lessons of Anant's past life continued to influence him, even if he was not always consciously aware of them. The knowledge of his previous existence as Vikram Singh, the corrupt bureaucrat, was not at the forefront of his mind, but it manifested in subtle ways—in his aversion to corruption, in his deep commitment to honesty and integrity, and in his unwavering sense of responsibility to those he served.

Anant often found himself reflecting on the nature of power and its potential to corrupt. He was acutely aware of the dangers of ambition, of the temptation to use one's position for personal gain rather than for the greater good. These reflections served as a constant reminder to stay true to his values, to never lose sight of the reasons he had chosen this path in the first place.

As he grew older and more experienced, Anant's

reputation as a principled and dedicated leader began to spread beyond the university. He was known not only for his intelligence and eloquence but also for his humility and compassion. People gravitated toward him, inspired by his vision and his commitment to creating a more just and equitable society.

Despite the praise and recognition he received, Anant remained humble. He knew that his work was far from finished and that the challenges he faced were immense. But he also knew that he was not alone. He was surrounded by like-minded individuals who shared his vision, and together, they formed a movement—a movement dedicated to fighting for justice, equality, and the rights of the marginalized.

**A New Beginning**

After graduating from university, Anant faced a critical decision. He could have taken a well-paying job in the private sector, or he could have pursued a career in politics, using his popularity and influence to climb the ranks of power. But Anant knew that neither of these paths was right for him. He had seen firsthand the dangers of power and wealth, and he was determined to avoid the pitfalls that had led him astray in his past life.

Instead, Anant chose to return to his roots, to the village where he had been raised. He knew that the real work of change began at the grassroots level, in the communities that were often overlooked and forgotten by those in power. He wanted to use his education and experience to uplift those who were struggling, to empower them to take control of their own lives and destinies.

When Anant returned to the village, he was greeted with open arms. The villagers, who had always seen him as one of their own, welcomed him back with warmth and gratitude. They knew that Anant was different, that he had the knowledge and skills to make a real difference in their lives, and they were eager to work with him to create a better future.

Anant wasted no time in getting to work. He began by organizing community meetings, where he listened to the concerns and needs of the villagers. He worked with them to identify the most pressing issues—access to clean water, education, healthcare, and economic opportunities—and together, they developed a plan to address these challenges.

One of Anant's first projects was to establish a cooperative, where the villagers could pool their resources and work together to improve their livelihoods. He helped them secure funding and training, and soon, the cooperative was thriving, providing the villagers with a stable source of income and a sense of pride in their work.

Anant also focused on education, recognizing that it was the key to breaking the cycle of poverty and empowering the next generation. He worked with local teachers to improve the quality of education in the village school, and he established a scholarship fund to help students pursue higher education. Under his guidance, the school became a model of excellence, and the students began to excel in their studies. Healthcare was another priority for Anant. He knew that many of the villagers suffered from preventable diseases due to a lack of access to medical care. He organized health camps and brought in doctors and nurses to provide free check-ups and treatment. He also worked to improve sanitation and hygiene in the village, reducing the spread of disease and improving overall health.

As the years passed, Anant's efforts began to bear fruit. The village transformed, becoming a vibrant and thriving community where people had access to the resources they needed to live healthy and productive lives. The villagers were empowered, taking an active role in their own development and working together to build a better future.

But Anant's impact extended beyond the village. Word of his work spread, and soon, other villages and communities were reaching out to him for help. He traveled across the region, sharing his knowledge and experience, helping to establish cooperatives, improve schools, and provide healthcare in other underserved areas. His work became a model for grassroots development, and he was recognized as a leader in the movement for social justice and rural development.

**The Test of Integrity**

Despite his success, Anant remained vigilant

against the dangers of power and corruption. He knew that the work he was doing would inevitably attract the attention of those who sought to exploit it for their own gain. He had seen how easily power could corrupt, how quickly good intentions could be twisted by greed and ambition.

One day, a wealthy landowner approached Anant with an offer. The landowner was impressed by the success of Anant's projects and wanted to invest in the cooperative. He offered a large sum of money in exchange for a controlling stake in the cooperative, promising to expand the business and bring in even greater profits.

But Anant knew better. He recognized the landowner's true intentions—he wanted to take control of the cooperative for his own benefit, to exploit the villagers and turn their hard work into his own personal wealth. Anant politely declined the offer, explaining that the cooperative was a community initiative and that its success depended on the collective ownership and control of the villagers.

The landowner was not pleased. He tried to

pressure Anant, offering even more money and promising to share the profits with him personally. But Anant stood firm, refusing to compromise his principles for the sake of wealth or power. He knew that accepting the offer would betray the trust of the villagers and undermine everything he had worked so hard to build.

Word of Anant's refusal spread, and it only strengthened his reputation as a man of integrity and principle. The villagers, who had heard of the landowner's offer, were grateful for Anant's steadfastness and were even more committed to working with him to improve their lives.

But the incident also served as a reminder of the challenges that Anant would continue to face. The path of service was not an easy one, and there would always be those who sought to take advantage of his work for their own gain. But Anant was prepared for these challenges, guided by the lessons of his past life and the commitment to truth and justice that had brought him to this point.

A Legacy of Service

As the years went by, Anant's work continued

to grow and evolve. He became a mentor to young people in the village, teaching them the values of honesty, integrity, and service. He encouraged them to pursue education and to use their knowledge to help others. Many of the young people he mentored went on to become leaders in their own right, carrying forward the work that Anant had begun.

Anant also became involved in broader efforts to bring about social and economic change. He worked with other grassroots leaders and activists to advocate for policies that supported rural development, education, and healthcare. He spoke at conferences and workshops, sharing his experiences and insights with others who were working to create a more just and equitable society.

But despite the recognition and success he achieved, Anant remained humble and focused on the work that still needed to be done. He knew that the path of service was a lifelong journey, one that required constant vigilance, dedication, and a willingness to put the needs of others before his own.

In his later years, Anant reflected on the journey

that had brought him to this point. He remembered the trials he had faced in Naraka, the lessons he had learned from the Light of Satya, and the choice of rebirth that had given him a second chance to live a life of virtue and righteousness. He was grateful for the opportunity to make amends for his past mistakes, to use his knowledge and experience to serve others and to create a legacy of service that would continue long after he was gone.

Anant's work had a lasting impact on the lives of countless people, but it was not the recognition or accolades that mattered to him. What mattered was the knowledge that he had lived a life true to his values, a life dedicated to the service of others, a life that honored the lessons he had learned through his journey of redemption.

As he looked out over the village that had become his home, Anant felt a deep sense of peace. He knew that he had fulfilled the purpose of his rebirth, that he had lived a life of meaning and integrity. And as he prepared to face the next chapter of his existence, whatever it might be, he did so with the knowledge that he had made a positive difference in the world—a difference that would continue to resonate for generations to come.

**Epilogue: A Cautionary Tale for India**

The story of Vikram Singh, a man who once wielded immense power and influence as a high-ranking bureaucrat in India, is a tale that transcends time and place. It is a story of moral reckoning, spiritual transformation, and the ultimate realization that true power lies not in wealth or authority, but in living a life of honesty, integrity, and service to others. As we bring this narrative to its close, it is essential to reflect on the lessons it offers, particularly for those who currently hold positions of power within the Indian government and society at large.

In a country as vast and diverse as India, where the challenges of governance are as complex as they are numerous, the temptation to succumb to corruption, greed, and the abuse of power is ever-present. The narrative of Vikram Singh serves as a poignant reminder that while it may be possible to evade earthly justice for a time, the divine consequences of one's actions are inescapable. The story illustrates that every choice, every action, carries with it a weight that will eventually be accounted for—whether in this life or the next.

**The Illusion of Power**

For many in positions of authority, power can become a seductive illusion, promising control, influence, and a sense of superiority over others. It is easy to forget that this power is not inherent but is granted by the people whom one is supposed to serve. Vikram Singh's life, as depicted in this tale, shows how this illusion of power can lead to moral decay. Once a man with noble intentions, he allowed his position to corrupt his soul, making decisions that served his own interests rather than the public good.

In the corridors of power, where decisions are made that affect millions of lives, there is a constant danger of losing sight of the true purpose of governance. The story of Vikram Singh is a warning that when power is used to serve personal greed rather than the welfare of the people, it becomes destructive—not just to those who are governed, but to the soul of the one who wields it.

Vikram's journey through Naraka, the trials he faced, and his ultimate rebirth as Anant, a humble servant of the people, serve as a stark reminder that true leadership is not about dominance or control. It is about service, humility, and a commitment to the principles of dharma—the moral law that governs the universe. Those in positions of power must remember that their authority is not an end in itself, but a means to uplift society, to ensure justice, and to protect the most vulnerable.

**The Inescapable Law of Karma**

At the heart of this narrative is the concept of karma, a fundamental principle in Hindu philosophy that dictates that every action has a corresponding consequence. Vikram Singh's life, his moral failings, and the suffering he caused to others set into motion a chain of events that led to his eventual downfall. But his story does not end there. The law of karma is not merely punitive; it is also redemptive. It offers the opportunity for atonement and transformation, as seen in Vikram's journey through Naraka and his subsequent rebirth.

For those in positions of power, the story of

Vikram Singh should serve as a powerful reminder that no action goes unnoticed in the cosmic order. The wealth, status, and power accumulated through dishonest means may bring temporary satisfaction, but they also create a heavy karmic debt that must eventually be repaid. The suffering inflicted upon others for personal gain will inevitably return to the one who caused it, whether in this life or in a future existence.

The message is clear: those who abuse their power and betray the trust of the people they serve will ultimately face the consequences of their actions. The law of karma is impartial and inescapable, and it holds every individual accountable for their deeds. This understanding should inspire those in power to act with integrity, knowing that their actions today will shape their destiny tomorrow.

**The Call to Dharma**

India, a land steeped in spiritual tradition, has always revered the concept of dharma—a principle that embodies righteousness, justice, and moral duty. For those who govern, dharma should be the guiding force behind every decision, every policy, and every action. The story of Vikram Singh is a call to return to these ancient principles, to embrace dharma not as an abstract concept, but as a practical guide to leadership and governance.

In the context of modern India, where corruption and abuse of power are pervasive challenges, the lessons from Vikram Singh's life are more relevant than ever. The story urges those in power to reflect on their own actions, to consider whether they are living up to the ideals of dharma, and to recognize the profound impact their choices have on the lives of others.

Dharma is not merely about following the letter of the law; it is about upholding the spirit of justice, compassion, and truth.

It requires a deep commitment to serving the greater good, to putting the needs of the people above personal gain, and to acting with honesty and integrity at all times. For those in government, this means resisting the temptations of corruption, nepotism, and self-interest, and instead, striving to create a society that is fair, just, and equitable for all.

## The Responsibility of Leadership

Leadership in any form—whether in government, business, or society—carries with it immense responsibility. The power to influence the lives of others is a sacred trust, one that should never be taken lightly. Vikram Singh's story is a reminder that leadership is not about personal glory or the accumulation of wealth, but about serving others with humility and dedication.

In the context of India's government, this responsibility is even greater. The country's rich cultural and spiritual heritage demands that its leaders embody the highest principles of dharma. This means being vigilant against the forces of corruption, standing up for the rights of the marginalized, and ensuring that the policies and decisions made are in the best interests of the people.

The story of Vikram Singh is a cautionary tale for those who may be tempted to stray from this path. It is a reminder that while the allure of power and wealth may be strong, the consequences of misusing that power are far-reaching and ultimately self-destructive. True leadership requires not only the ability to make difficult decisions but also the moral courage to do what is right, even when it is not easy.

**A Vision for India's Future**

As India continues to grow and develop, the lessons from Vikram Singh's story offer a vision for the future—a future where leaders are guided by the principles of dharma, where power is used to uplift and empower rather than to oppress and exploit. This vision calls for a return to the values that have long been at the heart of Indian culture: honesty, integrity, compassion, and a deep commitment to justice.

For this vision to become a reality, it requires the collective effort of all those in positions of power. It requires leaders who are willing to put the needs of the people above their own ambitions, who are committed to creating a society where everyone has the opportunity to thrive, and who understand that their actions today will shape the future of the nation.

The story of Vikram Singh is not just a tale of one man's journey; it is a reflection of the challenges and choices that face every leader. It is a reminder that the true measure of success is not the wealth or power one accumulates, but the positive impact one has on the lives of others.

**Embracing the Path of Service**

The narrative of Vikram Singh ultimately comes full circle, illustrating that the path to true fulfillment and peace lies not in the pursuit of power or wealth, but in the service of others. Vikram's rebirth as Anant, a humble servant of the people, represents the culmination of his journey—a journey that teaches us that the greatest leaders are those who lead by example, who serve with humility, and who remain steadfast in their commitment to justice and truth.

For those in positions of power, the story is a call to embrace the path of service, to recognize that true leadership is not about being served, but about serving others. It is about using one's position to create positive change, to uplift those who are struggling, and to ensure that the principles of dharma are upheld in every aspect of governance.

This path is not an easy one, and it requires

constant vigilance, self-reflection, and a willingness to make difficult choices. But it is the only path that leads to true fulfillment, to a life that is rich in meaning and purpose, and to a legacy that will endure long after one's time in power has come to an end.

**A Final Reflection**

As we conclude this narrative, it is important to reflect on the broader implications of Vikram Singh's story for India as a nation. India is a country with a deep spiritual heritage, a land where the principles of dharma have been revered for millennia. But it is also a country facing significant challenges—corruption, inequality, and social injustice—that threaten to undermine the very fabric of its society.

The story of Vikram Singh is a reminder that these challenges can only be overcome if those in power are willing to embrace the principles of dharma and to lead with integrity and compassion. It is a call to action for all those who hold positions of authority, urging them to reflect on their own actions, to consider the impact of their decisions, and to commit to serving the greater good.

The legacy of Vikram Singh, reborn as Anant, is a legacy of redemption—a reminder that it is never too late to change, to atone for past mistakes, and to live a life that is true to the highest ideals. It is a legacy that calls on all of us, regardless of our position or status, to live in accordance with the principles of dharma, to act with honesty and integrity, and to serve others with compassion and dedication.

As India moves forward, let us take the lessons of this story to heart. Let us strive to create a society where justice, equality, and truth are upheld, where power is used to uplift rather than to oppress, and where the principles of dharma guide every aspect of our lives.

In doing so, we can ensure that the story of Vikram Singh serves not just as a cautionary tale, but as an inspiration—a reminder that the path to true fulfillment lies in living a life of service, a life that honors the principles of dharma, and a life that leaves a positive and lasting impact on the world.

## Conclusion

Reflection on the Narrative and Its Lessons

The journey of Vikram Singh, as depicted in this book, is a profound exploration of the moral and spiritual consequences of corruption. It is a story that delves deep into the complexities of human nature, the temptations of power, and the enduring struggle between right and wrong. As we come to the conclusion of this narrative, it is essential to reflect on the lessons it offers—not just for the characters within the story, but for all of us who navigate the often murky waters of life's moral challenges.

At its heart, this narrative is a cautionary tale, one that reminds us of the dangers of losing sight of our moral compass. Vikram Singh's journey from a powerful bureaucrat to a soul tormented by the consequences of his actions serves as a powerful allegory for the importance of integrity, humility, and service in leadership. His story is a stark reminder that the choices we make have far-reaching consequences—not just in the immediate present, but in the long arc of our spiritual journey.

One of the most compelling aspects of Vikram's story is the way it forces us to confront the true cost of corruption. It is easy to see corruption as a victimless crime, or as a necessary evil in a complex and competitive world. However, this narrative strips away those justifications, revealing the human toll that corruption takes—the lives ruined, the trust shattered, and the opportunities lost. Through Vikram's trials in Naraka, we see that corruption is not just a violation of the law; it is a violation of the very principles that make us human.

But this story is not just about punishment and retribution. It is also about the possibility of redemption. Vikram's journey is one of transformation, where he moves from a place of darkness and despair to one of understanding, repentance, and ultimately, renewal. This process of redemption is not easy, nor is it guaranteed. It requires a deep and sincere commitment to change, a willingness to face the consequences of one's actions, and the courage to seek forgiveness and make amends.

For those in positions of power, Vikram's story is a reminder of the responsibilities that come with authority. Power is not an end in itself; it is a means to serve others and to promote the common good.

When power is used for personal gain, it becomes corrupt, and the consequences are devastating—not just for the individual, but for society as a whole. However, when power is wielded with integrity, compassion, and a commitment to justice, it can be a force for tremendous good.

As we reflect on Vikram Singh's journey, we are also reminded of the importance of dharma—the moral law that governs the universe. Dharma is not just a set of rules to follow; it is a guiding principle that informs every aspect of our lives. It is the force that keeps us aligned with our higher purpose, ensuring that our actions are in harmony with the greater good. For Vikram, the abandonment of dharma was the root of his downfall, and his journey through Naraka was a process of rediscovering and realigning with this essential principle.

This narrative also invites us to consider the concept of karma—the idea that every action has a corresponding consequence. Karma is not just a system of rewards and punishments; it is a mechanism of accountability, ensuring that we are held responsible for our actions. Vikram's experiences in the afterlife are a vivid illustration of this principle, as he is forced to confront the full impact of his choices. But karma also offers the possibility of redemption, allowing us to learn from our mistakes and to change our course before it is too late.

The Intersection of Mythology and Reality

One of the most intriguing aspects of this book is the way it weaves together elements of mythology and reality, creating a narrative that is both timeless and deeply relevant to contemporary life. By drawing on the rich traditions of Hindu mythology, the story of Vikram Singh becomes more than just a moral fable; it becomes a universal allegory that speaks to the human condition across cultures and epochs.

Hindu mythology is replete with stories that explore the themes of power, corruption, justice, and redemption. The characters of Yama, Chitragupta, and the various realms of Naraka are not just figures of myth; they are embodiments of the moral and spiritual forces that govern our lives. By placing Vikram Singh within this mythological framework, the narrative gains a depth and resonance that extends beyond the specifics of his story. It invites readers to see their own lives reflected in the trials and challenges that Vikram faces, and to consider the broader implications of their actions.

However, this intersection of mythology and reality is not just a literary device; it is also a commentary on the enduring relevance of these ancient stories. In a world that is increasingly driven by materialism and self-interest, the wisdom of the past offers a valuable counterpoint, reminding us of the importance of spiritual values and ethical principles. The story of Vikram Singh is a reminder that the lessons of mythology are not confined to the distant past; they are as relevant today as they ever were.

This narrative also challenges us to think about the ways in which we engage with mythology in our daily lives. In a modern, secular society, it is easy to dismiss these stories as mere superstition or folklore. However, this book suggests that mythology has a deeper purpose—one that goes beyond entertainment or moral instruction.

Mythology serves as a bridge between the material and the spiritual, the individual and the collective, the past and the future. It helps us to make sense of the complexities of life, offering insights that are both timeless and adaptable to the changing world.

For readers who may be unfamiliar with Hindu mythology, this book serves as an introduction to some of its most important concepts and characters. It invites readers to explore the rich tapestry of stories and symbols that have shaped Indian culture for millennia, and to consider how these ancient wisdom traditions can inform their own lives. For those who are already familiar with these traditions, the narrative offers a fresh perspective, reinterpreting familiar themes in a way that resonates with contemporary concerns.

But beyond its mythological elements, this narrative also engages with the reality of modern India. It is a story that reflects the challenges and contradictions of a rapidly changing society—one that is grappling with the legacy of colonialism, the pressures of globalization, and the ongoing struggle to define its identity in the 21st century. Through the lens of Vikram Singh's story, we are invited to consider the broader social and political context in which corruption flourishes, and to think critically about the forces that shape our lives.

The Ongoing Challenge of Corruption in Modern India

As we move from the realm of mythology to the reality of modern India, it is clear that the issues explored in this narrative are not just matters of individual morality; they are also deeply embedded in the structures and institutions of society. Corruption in India is not merely the result of personal failings; it is a systemic problem that affects every level of government, business, and civil society.

The story of Vikram Singh serves as a microcosm of the broader challenges facing India today. His journey reflects the experiences of countless individuals who have been seduced by the allure of power and wealth, only to find themselves trapped in a web of deceit and moral compromise. But it also reflects the experiences of those who suffer as a result of this corruption—the farmers driven to despair, the families torn apart by injustice, the children deprived of education and opportunity.

The impact of corruption on Indian society is profound. It distorts economic policies, undermines public trust, and perpetuates social inequalities. It creates a culture of cynicism and apathy, where people come to believe that the system is irredeemably corrupt and that individual actions cannot make a difference. This, in turn, leads to a vicious cycle, where corruption becomes normalized, and those who seek to challenge it are often marginalized or silenced.

However, the narrative of Vikram Singh also offers hope. It suggests that change is possible, even in the face of overwhelming odds. Through his journey of redemption, Vikram shows us that it is never too late to turn back, to make amends, and to realign with the principles of dharma. His story is a call to action for all of us—to resist the temptations of corruption, to hold ourselves and others accountable, and to work toward creating a more just and equitable society.

In the context of modern India, this call to

action is more urgent than ever. The challenges of corruption, inequality, and social injustice are not just abstract issues; they are realities that affect the daily lives of millions of people. Addressing these challenges requires a concerted effort from all sectors of society—government officials, business leaders, civil society organizations, and ordinary citizens.

For those in positions of power, the story of Vikram Singh is a reminder of the responsibilities that come with authority. It is a call to lead with integrity, to prioritize the common good over personal gain, and to create policies and institutions that are transparent, accountable, and fair. It is also a reminder that true leadership is not about accumulating power, but about using that power to serve others and to create a more just society.

For ordinary citizens, the narrative is a reminder of the power they hold in shaping the future of their country. Democracy is not just about casting a vote; it is about participating in the civic life of the nation, holding leaders accountable, and demanding transparency and justice. It is about resisting the normalization of corruption, speaking out against injustice, and working together to create a society where everyone has the opportunity to thrive.

The fight against corruption is not an easy one, and it will not be won overnight. But the story of Vikram Singh offers a roadmap for how we can begin to address these challenges. It shows us that change starts with the individual—with each of us making a commitment to live with integrity, to uphold the principles of dharma, and to hold ourselves accountable for our actions.

But it also shows us that change is possible on a broader scale—through collective action, through the creation of just and transparent institutions, and through the cultivation of a culture of accountability and ethical leadership.

### A Vision for the Future

As we conclude this book, it is important to look forward—to consider how the lessons of Vikram Singh's story can inform our vision for the future of India. The challenges facing the country are immense, but so too are the opportunities. India is a nation with a rich cultural heritage, a vibrant democracy, and a dynamic economy.

It is a country with a deep spiritual tradition that offers valuable insights into the nature of power, justice, and morality.

The story of Vikram Singh is a reminder that India's future will be shaped not just by its economic and political policies, but by the moral and ethical choices made by its leaders and citizens. It is a call to embrace the principles of dharma, to resist the temptations of corruption, and to work together to create a society that is fair, just, and equitable for all.

In this vision for the future, there is a place for everyone—whether you are a government official, a business leader, a civil society activist, or an ordinary citizen. Each of us has a role to play in building a better India, and each of us has the power to make a difference.

The choices we make today will determine the legacy we leave for future generations, and it is up to us to ensure that this legacy is one of integrity, justice, and compassion.

As we move forward, let us do so with the lessons

of Vikram Singh's story in mind. Let us remember that true power lies not in wealth or authority, but in the ability to make a positive difference in the lives of others. Let us commit to living in accordance with the principles of dharma, and to creating a society where justice, truth, and compassion prevail.

This book is not just a story; it is a call to action—a call to awaken the conscience of a nation, to remind us of the values that have sustained India for millennia, and to inspire us to build a better, brighter future for generations to come.

www.ingramcontent.com/pod-product-compliance
Lightning Source LLC
LaVergne TN
LVHW031343150826
845673LV00009B/2844
* 9 7 8 9 3 4 8 0 3 7 4 9 7 *